Communications
in Computer and Information Science 1412

More information about this series at http://www.springer.com/series/7899

Yichuan Wang · William Yu Chung Wang ·
Zhijun Yan · Dongsong Zhang (Eds.)

Digital Health and Medical Analytics

Second International Conference, DHA 2020
Beijing, China, July 25, 2020
Revised Selected Papers

 Springer

Editors
Yichuan Wang ⓘ
The University of Sheffield
Sheffield, UK

William Yu Chung Wang
University of Waikato
Hamilton, New Zealand

Zhijun Yan ⓘ
Beijing Institute of Technology
Beijing, China

Dongsong Zhang ⓘ
University of North Carolina at Charlotte
Charlotte, NC, USA

ISSN 1865-0929   ISSN 1865-0937   (electronic)
Communications in Computer and Information Science
ISBN 978-981-16-3630-1   ISBN 978-981-16-3631-8   (eBook)
https://doi.org/10.1007/978-981-16-3631-8

This Springer imprint is published by the registered company Springer Nature Singapore Pte Ltd.
The registered company address is: 152 Beach Road, #21-01/04 Gateway East, Singapore 189721, Singapore

Preface

The healthcare sector has experienced a significant transformation in past years, due to the digitalization of the healthcare service and ecosystem. Digitalization refers to the socio-technical process of utilizing digital technologies to catalyze the connectivity of individuals, organizations, industries, and society as a whole. Technologies including the Internet of Medical Things (IoMT), artificial intelligence (AI), medical analytics, wearable medical devices, blockchain, cloud computing, 3D/4D printing, and augmented and virtual reality hold the promise of liberating personal health data and offering a more cost-effective way of developing predictive, preventive, personalized, and participatory (P4) medicine.

With the rapid development of digitalization in healthcare, massive amounts of digital health data are now stored in medical information systems, which could be a valuable source for supporting healthcare organizations' clinical practices and operations, public health management, and medical research if it is analyzed in meaningful ways. However, despite the prosperity of digitalization in healthcare, this transformation comes with many challenges related to healthcare infrastructure, ecosystems, policy, ethics, and management. Obstacles include the lack of health data integration, data overload issues, data privacy and security, and limited or inefficient data visualization. As a result, there is an urgent need for further research to technologically explore how to utilize digital health data to support evidence-based medicine using data analytics approaches and to demonstrate how big data analytics and AI can enable healthcare practitioners and policy makers to sufficiently address societal health concerns and challenges.

The International Conference on Digital Health and Medical Analytics (DHA), co-founded by Dr. Yichuan Wang (University of Sheffield, UK) and Dr. William Yu Chung Wang (University of Waikato, New Zealand), has been collaborating with the University of Bristol (UK), Brandeis University (USA), the Kyushu Institute of Technology (Japan), the First Affiliated Hospital of Zhengzhou University (China), the Beijing Institute of Technology (China), and the University of North Carolina at Charlotte (USA). The aim of International Conference on Digital Health and Medical Analytics (DHA) is to bring together a wide spectrum of researchers, industry/start-up professionals, and healthcare practitioners to discuss multidisciplinary subjects including practice and social networks, analytics and engagement with health devices, big data, public health surveillance, persuasive technologies, epidemic intelligence, participatory surveillance, emergency medicine, serious games for public health interventions, and automated early identification of health threats and responses. Since its inception in 2017, the DHA conference has been an interdisciplinary gathering of researchers at the intersection of public health, information systems, healthcare management, and operation management. The first DHA conference was held in Zhengzhou, China (23–25 August 2019). The second DHA conference was held virtually on 25 July 2020.

This volume consists of research papers that were presented at DHA 2020, which took place on July 25th, 2020. Each paper underwent at least two rounds of reviews and revisions. These papers highlight the role of digitalization in the context of healthcare in regions including America, Europe, Asia, and Oceania. Case studies, surveys, and text mining approaches were utilized to investigate this phenomenon. This collection of research papers presents new insights contributing to the theory and practices in the digital health and medical analytics domains.

The proceedings editors wish to thank the dedicated conference Program Committee members, the International Advisory Committee members and all the reviewers for their contributions. We also thank Springer for their trust and for publishing the proceedings of DHA 2020.

March 2021   Yichuan Wang
                                                                          William Yu Chung Wang
                                                                                          Zhijun Yan
                                                                                  Dongsong Zhang

Organization

Conference Co-chairs

Zhijun Yan   Beijing Institute of Technology, China
William Wang   University of Waikato, New Zealand
Yichuan Wang   University of Sheffield, UK
Dongsong Zhang   University of North Carolina at Charlotte, USA

Program Co-chairs

Shiwei Sun   Beijing Institute of Technology, China
Minhao Zhang   University of Bristol, UK
Lin Jia   Beijing Institute of Technology, China
Luke Younghoon Chang   Beijing Institute of Technology, China
Qiuju Yin   Beijing Institute of Technology, China

Program Committee

Huigang Liang (Chair)   East Carolina University, USA
Guodong Gao   University of Maryland, College Park, USA
Changyong Liang   Hefei University of Technology, China
Jiye Mao   Renmin University of China, China
Yong Tan   University of Washington, USA
Kanliang Wang   Renmin University of China, China
Kang Xie   Sun Yat-Sen University, China
Han Zhang   Georgia Institute of Technology, USA
Pengzhu Zhang   Shanghai Jiao Tong University, China
Zhiqiang Zheng   University of Texas at Dallas, USA
Qinghua Zhu   Nanjing University, China

International Advisory Committee

Terry Byrd   Auburn University, USA
Wantao Yu   Roehampton University, UK
Xiaojun Wang   University of Bristol, UK
Jiang Yu   University of Chinese Academy of Sciences, China
Lincoln C. Wood   University of Otago, New Zealand
Stuart Dillon   Waikato University, New Zealand
Steven Hsiao   Rowan University, USA
Yen-Yo Wang   Auburn University, USA
Nick Hajli   Swansea University, UK
Mina Tajvidi   Newcastle University, UK

Zhen He	University of York, UK
Tianan Yang	Beijing Institute of Technology, China
Dongmei Cao	Coventry University, UK
Tingting Zhang	University of Science and Technology Beijing, China
Lincoln Wood	University of Otago, New Zealand
Lujie Chen	Xi'an Jiaotong-Liverpool University, China
Sena Ozdemir	Coventry University, UK
Roberta Bernardi	University of Bristol, UK
Huimin Lu	Kyushu Institute of Technology, Japan

Contents

A CNN-Based Method for Depression Detecting Form Audio

Shuangshuang Zhao, Qingqing Li, Chenbin Li, Yu Li, and Ke Lu[✉]

Anhui University of Technology, Maanshan 243032, China

Abstract. Depression, a major mental illness, has widely affected lives all over the world. Being depressed not only affects patients' mood, but also has a negative impact on patients' physical and mental health. It may lead to the lack of enthusiasm for daily life, low mental state, anxiety, irritability, anger and even suicidal tendencies. As the need to automatically detect depression using machine learning algorithms increases, an automatic depression detection method based on audio files and convolutional neural network (CNN) is proposed in this paper. First of all, we delete long silent sections of each audio file and splice the rest into a brand-new one. After that, add the label which represents if the participant is healthy or not to each file. Then, Mel frequency cepstrum coefficients (MFCCs), the features of speech signal, are extracted into matrix vector feature to represent the particular characteristics of participants' own voice. Eventually, the features are imported into the convolutional neural network model to complete the model training and evaluation. The results on Distress Analysis Interview Corpus-Wizard of Oz (DAIC-WOZ) dataset show that the overall prediction accuracy is 0.85, and the average probability of correct prediction of a single file is 0.82.

Keywords: Depression detecting · Deep learning · CNN · Audio · MFCC

1 Introduction

As a common and serious mental illness, depression can affect psychological and even physical health of the patient's daily life. It may causes feelings of sadness, pessimism, and impatience, changes in appetite, the loss of passions for life and so on. The World Health Organization (WHO) reports that 332 million people worldwide suffer from depression [1].

Although it is treatable, it is still necessary to detect this medical illness as early as possible. Different from other illness, traditional depression analysis methods are mainly dependent on people's verbal report, or behaviors reported by relatives or friends. Some mental status examinations, such as Beck Depression Inventory (BDI-II) [2], Hamilton Rating Scale for Depression (HRSD) [3] and Assessment of Negative Symptoms (SANS) [4], are contributed to depression detection. However, these methods mentioned above commonly based on subjective ratings with extensive medical expertise. Remote diagnose is not feasible either. Meanwhile, various factors tend to affect the rating result, e.g., testing time environment, and even the doctors who talked with patients.

© Springer Nature Singapore Pte Ltd. 2021
Y. Wang et al. (Eds.): DHA 2020, CCIS 1412, pp. 1–10, 2021.
https://doi.org/10.1007/978-981-16-3631-8_1

What's more, an easily overlooked consequence is that detecting frequently may cause heavy mental burden to both patients and psychological doctors. Time consuming the fluctuation of detecting result and the support of individual cause an automatic or semi-automatic diagnosis method is required. Although depression may cause the changes of body characteristics index, e.g., blood pressure and body weight, it is impossible to detect depression based on any physical examination. Since depression people behave different from normal people, detecting depression through audio and video of person has drawn increasing attention recently [5–7]. The audio of depressed people may imply some subtle difference that can help detecting depression. Hence much efforts have been dedicated to diagnose based the audio collected. For example, the speaker's speech signal and its internal emotional and psychological activities are analyzed by automatic speech depression detection. There are two types of methods for automatic detection of depression, deep learning-based methods and traditional machine learning methods, in existing research [8]. In recent years, deep learning models based on neural network models for extracting advanced semantic features have made considerable progress [9, 10].

Especially in Audio-Visual Emotion Challenge (AVEC), a competition related to detecting depression based audio, researches from different disciplines have attempted to utilize various methods to detecting depression based on audio [11–13]. Dham et al. applied Gaussian Mixture Model (GMM) clustering and Fisher vector approach based on the visual data [14]. Wang et al. proposed a speech depression detection mechanism by using CNN and generating adversarial network model [15]. And a framework for detecting depression based on deep recurrent neural networks is presented, and it also predicts the severity of depression patients based on the characteristics of audio files [16]. Although many attempts have been dedicated to detecting depression based on audio with neural network, existing methods tag a sample with a single audio file during training and finally output the total prediction accuracy without the probability of correct prediction for a single file.

This paper addresses the issue mentioned above and proposes a novel method to diagnose depression. Our method is based on the known mental health of the participants to add a label that distinguishes whether they have got into depression or not. We assume that every frame of the voice file of a depressed patient is depressed. After de-silencing the audio files and training these inputs through convolutional neural network. The prediction accuracy for a single file is finally obtained according to the ratio of the correct frame predicted in a single file. The basic knowledge of our method are introduced in Sect. 2. The details of our method will be described in Sect. 3. In Sect. 4, we introduce the experimental process in detail and discussed the results. The summary of this paper is in Sect. 5.

2   Preliminaries

Experiments show that human hearing perception will focus on a special audio city, above or below its frequency domain, humans cannot perceive their audio. Human hearing is like a filter bank, and after filtering it leaves behind identifiable information. The Mel scale is a non-linear frequency scale set by the human ear for the sensory judgment of equidistant pitch changes, which is similar with human hearing characteristics and has low dimensions. Therefore, in the processing of voice signals, MFCC features are widely used [17].

2.1 Mel Frequency Cepstrum Coefficient

In audio processing, MFCCs can effectively combine the auditory perception character-istics of the human ear with the speech signal generation mechanism. The Mel filters are used to process voice signal. And the Mel filters are actually a row of non-linear interval band-pass filters, whose frequency response design is similar to how the human cochlea handles frequency when listening to sound. A common frequency measured in Hertz (f) can be converted to the MFCCs frequency scale using the following formula:

$$f_{mel} = 25951 \log\left(1 + \frac{f_{H_z}}{700}\right) \tag{1}$$

In the above formula: f_{mel} expresses Mel frequency scale, f_{H_z} expresses common fre-quency. Converting the common frequency domain of the voice signal to the MFCCs fre-quency scale, which can better simulate the processing of the auditory process. To sum up, the calculation for MFCCs utilize a group of filters with triangular frequency response. Assuming that the number of filters is M, the filtered output is $X(m)$, $m = 1, 2, \ldots, M$; and set $h(m), c(m), l(m)$ be the upper limit frequency, center frequency and lower limit frequency of m triangular filters. The following formula explains the relation-ship between the upper limit, center and lower limit frequency of the adjacent triangle filter:

$$c(m) = h(m-1) = l(m+1) \tag{2}$$

The outputs of the filter bank are logarithmically operated, and then the inverse transform operation of discrete cosine is performed to achieve MFCCs:

$$C_n = \sum_{m-1}^{M} \log X(m) \cos\left((m - 0.5)\frac{n\Pi}{M}\right) n = 1, 2, \ldots, L \tag{3}$$

In formula (3), L is the coefficient of MFCCs. Generally, the number of filter M is between 20 and 40.

2.2 Network Description

As a classic model in deep learning, CNN is well known as a strong tool for theoretical and practical tasks, such as image processing and speech recognition [18–20]. Because of its shift invariant and the simplicity of its network structure, CNN has attracted a wide range of researchers.

In general, a typical CNN consists of similar structure in most common deep neural network, including convolutional layers, pooling layers and fully connected layers three parts. A convolution layer contains a convolution kernels to slide the input. In common input as a regular shape tensor pass through the convolution. But in order to improve the accuracy of the network, the network always composed of multiple convolution kernels to extract the deeper feature of the input. Pooling layer pays more attention to achieve dimension reduction. It always focus on certain features rather than the position of the features, and is used to compress the amount of data and parameters to relief over-fitting. Fully connected layers are used to connect each neuron of two different layers to achieve a transition from a fully connected layer to a flat matrix for better classification.

There are major distinguish features about convolution neural network. Firstly, the entire input area share convolution kernel when convolution neural network working. The share weights effectively decrease the number of parameters to be learned, then increasing the operation speed. In addition, CNN requires the spatial local correlation information by strengthening the local connection mode of nodes between adjacent layers in the neural network, which effectively reduces the complexity of the convolutional neural network model.

3 Depression Detection Model Based on CNN

In consideration of the deep features extracted by the neural network are superior to the low-dimensional features such as the traditional sound frequency, this paper attempts to extract and train the unique features related to depression in the human voice modality, and then predict whether there is depression in the test audio samples. The whole framework and key steps of the method will be described in detail below.

3.1 Method

Our method is based on the motivation described as following. When a patient is diagnosed for depression, a talk between a doctor and the patient is needed. It is assumed that the hints of depression are hidden in the patients' voice, and then we can detect depression based on finding the features related to depression from patients' audio file. For example, we can slide a patient's audio file into 1000 frames. If the depression features can be found from 800 frames among the total 1000 frames, it can be said that the possibility of patient to whom this audio file belong may be suffered from depression is 80%.

In this work, we first perform the de-mute process on the speech sample files, and then extract the low-dimensional features of these files. Finally, we send the features to the audio network framework used to detect depression for training and testing. The final experiment outputs the proportion of frames that we predicted correctly for each file, and the final overall prediction accuracy is obtained. The overall framework of the specific depression recognition method is shown in Fig. 1.

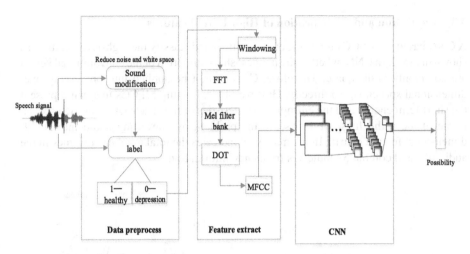

Fig.1. The whole framework of the depression detection method based on CNN and audio signals.

The specific work steps for identifying depression in this paper are:

Preprocess the first-hand audio files. Then delete the longer silent clips in each audio file, and splice the remaining clips into a rebuild one. After that, label each file for depression or health.

Extract the Mel frequency cepstrum coefficient of the speech signal. The extracted MFCCs are used to obtain the characteristic data of the participants' unique voice attributes. This is the vital data materials for the network model to complete normal training.

Input the features into the convolutional neural network model. Then get more representative features for completing the evaluation work.

3.2 Extraction of MFCC Features

The Mel frequency cepstrum coefficients are commonly extracted to describe voice features in speech detection because they are robust in representing low-frequency signal changes. The MFCCs can indicate the cepstrum energies with a nonlinear Mel-scale. In current speech recognition system, first extract MFCCs of the voice files to identify the components in the audio signal, and then refine the semantic content we need to use, also discard the irrelevant information. The processes of extracting MFCC features as follows. Firstly, pre-emphasize, frame and window the speech files. Then obtain the corresponding frequency spectrum from Fast Fourier Transformation (FFT) of each short-term analysis window. And pass the above spectrum through the Mel filter bank to get the Mel spectrum. Finally, achieve MFCCs by analyzing cepstrum on the Mel spectrum.

3.3 Acquisition and Classification of High-Level Features

A CNN based on MFCCs is constructed to extract and classify the high-level features as shown in Fig. 2. In CNN, whether the images' shape imported or the convolutional kernel are commonly both square. Therefore, CNN cannot be applied into processing one-dimensional speech signal directly. However, by extracting MFCCs that can represent the short-term energy and the entropy characteristics of the spectrogram in each speech frame of the audio files, we can solve the problem by converting audio into N*39-dimensional feature matrix. In the matrix, N indicates the total number of frames in the audio file, and column 39 indicates frequency information.

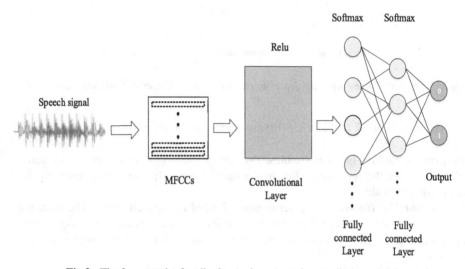

Fig.2. The framework of audio depression regression prediction model.

When processing the entire frequency, instead of using a square filter, we adopt a one-dimensional convolution. Convolutional layers will attain rich high-order semantic information from existing MFCCs. After the convolution process, we use Rectified Linear Unit (ReLu) as the activation function. For linear functions, its expression ability is stronger, above all in deep networks; for nonlinear functions, ReLu has a non-negative interval gradient, which is constant, so there is no problem of gradient disappearance, which keeps the convergence rate of the model at a stable state. The flat layer is used to flatten the entire matrix, thereby effectively realizing the connection between the convolutional layer and the fully connected layer. Finally, two fully connected layers for long-term coding make up the back end of the network structure.

4   Experiments and Discussions

4.1 Implementation Details

The experimental data set contains a total of 142 files, including 42 patients with depression and 100 healthy people. In order to improve the recognition performance and avoid over-fitting, we keep the proportion of depression in training set is 50%, the data distribution as shown in Table 1.

Table 1. The distribution of audio samples.

Dataset	Healthy individuals	Depressed individual
Training sets	25	25
Test sets	75	17

Preprocessing DAIC-WOZ sample to obtain representative features. When listening to the questions, the participants cannot produce any audio information. Therefore, the silent sections need to be cut off. First, we delete the longer mute segments of each audio file, and rebuild another audio file by splicing the rest sections. In our work, according to the difference in volume among of all audio files, the threshold is flexibly set to determine whether the current state is in a silent state, and then when the silent audio exceeds 1.5 s, the segment is removed. After that, a brand new file can be obtained by adding a blank segment with a length of 0.3 s at both ends of these audio segments.

According to the data set information on the official website, we add a label to each processed audio file, where 0 indicates health and 1 indicates depression. Then we extract the 39-dimensional MFCC features of audio files for training. Put the randomly selected training set file into the CNN model, which consists of a convolutional layer and two fully connected layers. In this work, we use softmax as the activation function, Adadelta is used as optimizer, and loss function is categorical crossentropy.

4.2 Depression Recognition Results

We set different batch sizes and different iterations to verify the stability of the model. At the same time determine the appropriate training times and batch size. The corresponding experimental results are described in Table 2. Considering comprehensively the efficiency and accuracy of prediction, we find that when the number of epochs is 100 and the batch size is 400, the model performs well.

The receiver operating characteristic (ROC) curve is a graphical diagram that illustrates the diagnostic capabilities of the binary classifier system when the discrimination threshold changes. In the work, we make a binary judgment on whether the participant has depression or is in health, then draw the ROC curve according to the experimental results achieved by setting different threshold of mental health standards. As is shown in Fig. 3, the abscissa is False Positive Rate (FPR) that meaning of the probability of false refusing the void hypothesis, and the ordinate is True positive Rate (TPR) can be interpreted which is correctly identified as the possibility of actual positives. The value Area Under Curve (AUC) is 0.78. At this time, the overall prediction accuracy of the model is 0.85, and the average probability of correct prediction of a single file is 0.82.

Table 2. The prediction accuracy obtained by using different batch sizes and different numbers of epochs.

Epochs	Batch size	Accuracy	Val accuracy
50	200	0.8319	0.8091
100	200	0.8413	0.8252
200	200	0.8451	0.8276
50	400	0.8325	0.8160
100	400	0.8478	0.8198
200	400	0.8622	0.8366
50	600	0.8316	0.8163
100	600	0.8516	0.8265
200	600	0.8609	0.8433

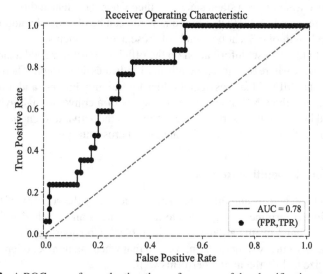

Fig.3. A ROC curve for evaluating the performance of the classification model.

5   Conclusion

This paper presents a method for automatically identifying depression based on MFCCs and convolutional neural networks. Our work assumes that every frame of an audio file of a depressive patient has a signal characteristic that shows a tendency to depression. After preprocessing the audio file, we put the labeled MFCC feature data into the convolutional neural network model to complete the training. The evaluations were carried out on DAIC-WOZ used for the AVEC 2017 competition. Final prediction accuracy for a single file was obtained according to the ratio of the correct frame predicted in a single file. In general, we attained an overall prediction accuracy of 0.86, and the average accuracy of a single file prediction is 0.84. When adjusting related training parameters, the model still has high stability and prediction accuracy which demonstrate the effectiveness of the proposed method.

References

1. Mathers, C., Boerma, J.T., Fat, D.M.: The global burden of disease: 2004 update. World Health Organization (2008)
2. Mcpherson, A., Martin, C.R.: A narrative review of the Beck Depression Inventory (BDI) and implications for its use in an alcohol-dependent population. Psychiatric Mental Health Nurs. **17**(1), 19–30 (2010)
3. Zimmerman, M., Chelminski, I., Posternak, M.: A review of studies of the Hamilton depression rating scale in healthy controls: implications for the definition of remission in treatment studies of depression. Nerv. Mental Disease **192**(9), 595–601 (2004)
4. Andreasen, N.C.: The scale for the assessment of negative symptoms (SANS): conceptual and theoretical foundations. Br. J. Psychiatry Suppl. **13**(7), 49–58 (1989)
5. Dham, S., Sharma, A., Dhall, A.: Depression scale recognition from audio, visual and text analysis. http://arxiv.org/abs/1709.05865 (2017)
6. Giannakopoulos, T., Smailis, C., Perantonis, S., et al.: Realtime depression estimation using mid-term audio features. In: Proceedings of CEUR Workshop, vol. 1213, pp. 41–46 (2014)
7. Hanai, T.A., Ghassemi, M., Glass, J.: Detecting depression with audio/text sequence modeling of interviews. In: Interspeech, pp. 1716–1720 (2018)
8. Vázquez-Romero, A., Gallardo-Antolín, A.: Automatic detection of depression in speech using ensemble convolutional neural networks. Entropy **22**, 688 (2020)
9. Cong, Q., Feng, Z., Li, F.: XA-BiLSTM: a deep learning approach for depression detection in imbalanced data. In: 2018 IEEE International Conference on Bioinformatics and Biomedicine BIBM, pp. 1624–1627 (2018)
10. Yang, L., Jiang, D., Xia, X., et al.: Multimodal measurement of depression using deep learning models. In: Proceedings of the 7th Annual Workshop on Audio/Visual Emotion Challenge, pp. 53–59. ACM (2017).
11. Mitra, V., Tsiartas, A., Shriberg, E.: Noise and reverberation effects on depression detection from speech. In: IEEE International Conference on Acoustics, pp. 5795–5799. IEEE (2016)
12. Yao, Z.-J., Bi, J., Chen, Y.-X.: Applying deep learning to individual and community health monitoring data: a survey. Int. J. Autom. Comput. **15**(6), 643–655 (2018). https://doi.org/10.1007/s11633-018-1136-9
13. Yang, L., Jiang, D.M., He, L., et al.: Decision tree based depression classification from audio video and language information. In: Proceedings of the 6th International Workshop on Audio/Visual Emotion Challenge, pp. 89–96. ACM (2016)
14. Dham S., Sharma A., Dhall A.: Depression scale recognition from audio, visual and text analysis. arxiv.org https://arxiv.org/abs/1709.05865 (2018)
15. Wang, Z., Chen, L., Wang, L., et al.: Recognition of audio depression based on convolutional neural network and generative antagonism network model. IEEE Access **8**, 101181–101191 (2020)
16. Rejaibi, E., Komaty, A., Meriaudeau, F., et al.: MFCC-based recurrent neural network for automatic clinical depression recognition and assessment from speech. PreprintarXiv:1909.07208 (2019)
17. Ma, X., Yang, H., Chen, Q., et al.: DepAudioNet: an efficient deep model for audio based depression classification. In: Proceedings of the 6th International Workshop on Audio/Visual Emotion Challenge, Co-located with ACM Multimedia 2016, pp. 35–42 (2016)

18. Huang, Z., Dong, M., Mao, Q., et al.: Speech emotion recognition using CNN. In: ACM International Conference on Multimedia, pp. 801–804. ACM (2014)
19. Huang, J.T., Li, J., Gong, Y.: An analysis of convolutional neural networks for speech recognition. In: Proceedings of the IEEE International Conference on Acoustics, Speech and Signal Processing (ICASSP), Australia, pp. 4989–4993 (2015)
20. Parcollet, T., Zhang, Y., Morchid, M., et al.: Quaternion convolutional neural networks for end-to-end automatic speech recognition. In: Interspeech (2018)

Design of Chinese Medicine Health Management System

Ruixiang Wang(✉) and Chunyan Wang

Shandong University of Traditional Chinese Medicine, Daxue Road 4655, Jinan, China

Abstract. For thousands of years, traditional Chinese medicine (TCM) ensured the health of the Chinese people in the most convenient way and at the lowest cost. TCM has formed a set of health management methods for preventing and controlling diseases. Contents of TCM health management include body constitution (BC) identification, disease prevention and treatment of TCM. The TCM health management system is a system that uses TCM's theory to intelligently identify health status and provide intervention suggestions. The TCM health management system cannot fully reflect the concepts and methods of TCM health management. This study designed a framework of TCM health management system. This system framework is designed from the perspective of TCM logic rather than technology. The designed system integrates BC identification, disease prevention and treatment of TCM, forming a logical chain of TCM health management. In China, TCM is an important part of the medical system. Therefore, the TCM health management system in line with the logic of TCM is expected to become a valuable supplement to the modern medical health management system.

Keywords: Traditional Chinese medicine · Health management system · Framework

1 Introduction

The development and progress of society have led to the growing demand for health, and the contradiction between the expanding health need and limited medical resources has become increasingly prominent. How to ensure that everyone enjoys health under the premise of limited resources has become a problem that every country must face.

At present, there are two kinds of medicine in China. One is modern medicine and the other is TCM. The introduction of modern medicine has significantly improved the average life expectancy of Chinese people and the health level of Chinese people. However, TCM health management methods have also proved their effectiveness and reliability in many years of clinical practice [1]. Through the observation of human physiological and pathological phenomena, TCM formed a set of self-consistent logical system. Under the guidance of this logic system, TCM ensured the health of the Chinese for thousands of years.

In the years of relying only on TCM, a literate person could achieve self-health management by learning TCM knowledge without strict medical training [2]. Therefore,

© Springer Nature Singapore Pte Ltd. 2021
Y. Wang et al. (Eds.): DHA 2020, CCIS 1412, pp. 11–17, 2021.
https://doi.org/10.1007/978-981-16-3631-8_2

in the information age, it is feasible to establish a TCM health management system based on the experience and knowledge of TCM.

The current research on TCM health management system is reflected in TCM BC recognition health management system and TCM diagnosis and treatment health management system [3, 4]. These studies have intelligently implemented TCM health management from different perspectives, and can provide health status identification and health consultation services to the population. These studies have focused more on the technical realization, but failed to establish a complete framework for TCM health management. They have not logically sorted out the relationship between BC and sub-health, sub-health and TCM disease prevention, TCM prevention and treatment. This article expounds the concepts of TCM BC, TCM sub-health, TCM disease prevention, TCM disease treatment and other concepts, discusses the inherent logical relationship of these concepts, and thus designs a service system framework of TCM health management.

2 Methods

The TCM health management system is a computer program that can intelligently recognize the health, sub-health and disease status of TCM with the assistance of modern medical diagnosis, and provide TCM intervention and treatment consulting services based on the recognition results.

2.1 Method of TCM BC Identification

TCM believes that the human body exists in three states: healthy state, sub-health state and disease state [5]. The state of the human body can be partially discerned by distinguishing the BC. The concept of BC is an important concept of TCM, which has been widely used in clinical diagnosis and treatment of TCM. TCM divides people into different types according to their BC. In the field of Chinese medicine, the classification method of BC is controversial. The current authoritative classification method is to divide people into gentleness BC, qi-deficiency BC, yang-deficiency BC, yin-deficiency BC, phlegm-wetness BC, wetness-heat BC, blood-stasis BC, qi-depression BC and special diathesis BC [6].

Factors to distinguish BC include multiple factors such as body shape, whether the skin is shiny, psychological conditions, and ability to adapt to the outside world. For example, a gentleness BC is a BC possessed by a healthy person, which is mainly characterized by a well-balanced shape, moisturized complexion, thick and shiny hair, cheerful personality, less illness, and strong adaptability to natural and social environments. Qi-deficiency constitution is usually characterized by poor health, shortness of breath, too lazy to talk, easy to fatigue, lack of energy, easy to sweat, introverted personality, emotional instability, easy to catch cold, poor immunity, etc. People with yang-deficiency tend to be fatter, colder, have cold hands and feet, sleep more, have tooth marks on their tongues, are introverted, and often grow sick due to cold.

TCM believes that people with a gentleness BC are healthy, and people with eight other BC belong to a sub-healthy state. The reasons for different BC include both innate factors and acquired factors. People with different BC have different susceptibility to different diseases. For example, people with qi-deficiency BC are more likely to catch a cold. People with phlegm-wetness BC are much more likely to suffer from hypertension, hyperlipidemia, coronary heart disease, and stroke than those with other BC. People with special diathesis BC are more likely to be allergic [7]. Through the investigation of personal BC, we will know whether the disease will occur, and what is the development trajectory after the disease occurs. If we can properly intervene in the state of sub-health, we can reduce the risk of illness to a certain extent.

In the work of [8], the author conducted a BC survey of 1084 Hong Kong residents. The survey results shows that 20.0% of people have a gentleness constitution, 56.2% of people have a constitution of Qi-deficiency, 39.0% of people have a constitution of Yang-deficiency, 40.7% of people have a constitution of Yin-deficiency, 41.2% of people have a phlegm-wetness constitution, 38.1% of people have a wetness-heat constitution, 40.1% of people have a blood-stasis constitution, 41.9% of people have a qi-depression constitution, 34.4% of people have a special diathesis constitution, 1.4% of people failed to discern what their BC are, 64.9% have more than one imbalanced constitution. The above survey results show that the BC differences between the people are objective, most residents are in a sub-healthy state, and a person can have more than one unbalanced constitution. At the same time, the survey shows that most people are in a sub-health state. Because modern medicine lacks effective treatment methods, Chinese medicine intervention is imperative.

The purpose of TCM identification of BC is to determine whether the consultant is in a sub-health state, which one or several sub-health states it is in, and what modern medical examinations are required to provide a basis for further TCM intervention.

2.2 Method of TCM Disease Prevention

Modern medicine generally achieves disease prevention by adjusting people's living habits. In the 60s and 70s of the 20th century, the mortality rate of cardiovascular diseases in Finland was particularly high, which seriously endangered the health of local people and consumed a lot of medical resources. Researchers have found that excessively high cholesterol levels are the key factor leading to a high incidence of cardiovascular disease in Finland, and excessively elevated cholesterol levels are inseparable from the native residents' eating habits. From the 1970s to the 1990s, through community intervention, the smoking rate of Finns decreased significantly, the consumption of butter decreased dramatically, and the consumption of vegetables increased dramatically, which directly leads to a drop in average cholesterol and blood pressure. As a result, the mortality rate from cardiovascular diseases has been reduced by 68%, the average life expectancy has increased by 6–7 years, and the goal of health management has been successfully achieved [9].

The goal of health management is to keep people in a healthy state. In traditional Chinese medicine, it is believed a excellent doctor can effectively cure sub-health state and keep physical fitness. Prevention of disease by TCM is reflected in two aspects. The first aspect is the intervention of the sub-healthy population, the purpose is to restore the health of the sub-healthy population; the second aspect is to use Chinese medicine to intervene before the disease occurs, so that the disease will not occur as much as possible.

For sub-healthy people, that is, those who often experience discomfort and cannot be diagnosed as a patient, modern medicine is often powerless, and TCM shows significant advantages. Sub-health refers to people with an unbalanced constitution based on TCM theory. "Clinical Guidelines for Sub-health Chinese Medicine" published by Chinese officials in 2004 described the concept of sub-health, the common symptoms of sub-health, the syndromes of TCM corresponding to the symptoms, the intervention methods of TCM for sub-health [10].

China is the one with the largest diabetes population. Studies have shown that when impaired fasting glucose (IGT) is low, it is very likely to develop into diabetes, but the low IGT cannot be used as a diagnostic basis for diabetes, it cannot be treated with drugs. Tong X used the traditional Chinese medicine prescription "Tianqi Jiangtang Capsule" for 420 IGT patients and used a randomized, double-blind test method. The results showed that it could reduce the impact of diabetes by 32.1%. The intervention of TCM for the early symptoms of the disease is mainly reflected in the few fields such as diabetes, hypertension [11, 12].

In summary, modern medicine attaches importance to the collection and analysis of biochemical indicators and pathological samples, and intervenes in advance in lifestyle habits and other factors that may cause diseases. TCM is a Chinese medicine-based intervention for sub-healthy people and pre-disease people. Therefore, prevention of diseases by TCM is a useful supplement for the prevention of diseases in modern medicine.

2.3 Method of TCM Disease Treatment

TCM does not have concepts such as hypertension and diabetes. Since the introduction of modern medicine into China, the thinking of TCM has undergone immense changes. At present, TCM clinics generally adopt a combination of disease and syndrome treatment, that is, to classify disease syndromes, and then carry out TCM intervention according to the syndrome type.

The key to TCM treatment of diseases lies in the judgment of patients' syndromes and the selection of treatment methods based on syndromes. The principle of TCM's identification of the patient's syndrome is the same as that of BC, which is judged according to the patient's symptoms. The syndrome is the foundation of TCM treatment of the disease. TCM treatment methods include soup, acupuncture, massage, and food therapy and so on.

2.4 Design Method of TCM Health Management System

Currently, there is no universally accepted definition of TCM health management system. Researchers constructed different systems according to their own understanding. In the work of [13], the authors built a human body constitution recognition system, which can realize automatic recognition of human body constitution. In the work of [14], the authors built a diagnosis and treatment system of TCM as a platform for health management.

3 Results

The TCM health management system is a supplement to the medical health management system. The TCM health management system can be used not only in communities or medical institutions, but also in providing individual health management consulting services. The TCM health management system should include three modules, the first module is a BC identification module, the second module is a disease prevention module, and the third module is a disease treatment module. The framework of the designed TCM health management system is shown in Fig. 1.

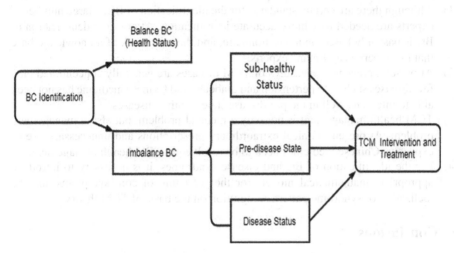

Fig. 1. TCM health management system framework.

Figure 1 shows that when a person is consulting, he needs to answer related questions, and the system determines the BC of the person. If the consultant is an unbalanced state, the system will derive the corresponding syndrome of the patient according to the TCM theory, and provide the consultant with different modern medical test suggestions according to the different syndromes. After conducting modern medical examinations, the consultants are divided into three categories according to the results. One category is the general sub-health state. The other category is the pre-disease state, and the other is the disease state. If the consultant is only in a general sub-health state, the system will give corresponding intervention suggestions such as food and Chinese medicine to allow the consultant to return to a healthy state. If the consultant is in a pre-disease state, it needs to be treated according to the experience of Chinese medicine to avoid the occurrence of the disease. If the consultant is in a disease state, the system needs to choose a proper Chinese medicine treatment method according to the need to treat the disease. Based on the theory of Chinese medicine, we have clearly defined the relationship between BC, sub-health, pre-disease and disease, which will help to transform the existing BC identification system and disease diagnosis and treatment system to form a complete TCM health management system.

4 Discussion

TCM is an empirical science, and the judgment of causality depends to some extent on the experience of experts. Therefore, whether it is the judgment of BC or syndromes, it is

16   R. Wang and C. Wang

based on the experience of a large number of Chinese medicine experts and appropriate mathematical models. Therefore, an ideal TCM health management system must be an assistant decision support system that brings together expert experience. At present, the TCM health management system has room for further improvement in the following points.

(1) Although there are certain standards for the identification of BC, a large number of experts are needed to achieve accurate identification. At present, identification of BC is basically based on a questionnaire, and there is a lack of a knowledge base that the experience of many experts.
(2) At present, preventive measures of TCM diseases are generally concentrated on a few diseases such as hypertension and diabetes, and Chinese medicine has not been able to intervene well in the pre-disease state of other diseases.
(3) TCM health management is not only a medical problem, but also a management problem. At present, clinical extraordinary prescriptions and unnecessary use of expensive Chinese medicines need to be resolved in TCM health management.
(4) For the identification of BC and disease syndromes, it is necessary to introduce appropriate mathematical models for the screening of core symptoms and the realization of syndrome pattern recognition on the basis of TCM theory.

5 Conclusions

TCM is playing an increasingly important role in China because of the localization of its thinking and its remarkable curative effect. Chinese medicine is committed to the identification of health status of the human body, the treatment of sub-health, the early diagnosis and treatment of diseases and the convenient method of treating diseases. TCM unifies disease prevention and treatment, food and medicine, personal unique BC and acquired intervention. TCM health management conforms to the requirements of the prevailing biomedical model with health as the core. The establishment of a TCM health management system that conforms to the logic of TCM is not simply the need for Chinese medical institutions, but also meets the individual need for TCM health management.

This study designed a framework of TCM health management system based on the elaboration of the connotation of TCM health management. This designed system organically combines the identification of TCM BC, modern medical examination, judgment of sub-health and pre-disease, TCM intervention of unbalanced BC, and treatment of diseases according to the logic of TCM. This research has laid a solid foundation for the development and application of TCM health management system.

Acknowledgments. This work is partially supported by Shandong Natural Science Foundation Project (ZR2017LH062) and Shandong Soft Science Research Project (2014RKB14161).

References

1. Zhang, X.: Comparison of Chinese and western medical methodology. J. Guangzhou Univ. Tradit. Chin. Med. **22**(05), 80–82 (2005)

2. Wang, J., Wang, J., Dai, E.: Su Shi and traditional Chinese medicine—also on the phenomenon of confucianism and knowledge of medicine in song dynasty. Guangming Tradit. Chin. Med. **35**(04), 487–489 (2020)
3. Li, C., Zhao, W., Xu, J.: Traditional Chinese medicine health management based on health state differentiation. China J. Tradit. Chin. Med. Pharm. **34**(2), 661–664 (2019)
4. Yang, X., Gan, H., Lai, X., et al.: Research and development of Chinese medicine health management system based on syndrome differentiation model. Chin. J. Tradit. Chin. Med. **30**(08), 2681–2683 (2015)
5. Jiang, L.: Preliminary exploration of the concepts related to health, sub-health, no disease and treatment of no disease. Chin. J. Tradit. Chin. Med. **25**(02), 167–170 (2020)
6. Wang, Q.: Classification and diagnosis basis of nine basic constitutions in Chinese medicine. J. Beijing Univ. Tradit. Chin. Med. **28**(04), 1–4 (2005)
7. Qian, H.: Discussing and analyzing prevention and cure strategy of traditional chinese medicine according to characteristic of sub-health condition. Chin. J. Tradit. Chin. Med. **21**(10), 589–591 (2006)
8. Wong, W.S., Lam, C.L., Wong, V.T., et al.: Validation of the constitution in Chinese medicine questionnaire: does the traditional Chinese medicine concept of body constitution exist? Evid.-Based Complement. Altern. Med. Spec. Issue 1–14 (2013)
9. Puska, P.: Successful prevention of non-communicable diseases: 25 year experiences with North Karelia Project in Finland. Publ. Health Med. **4**(01), 5–7 (2002)
10. Chinese Society of Traditional Chinese Medicine.: TCM constitution classification and judgment (ZYYXH/T157-2009). World J. Integr. Tradit. Chin. West. Med. **4**(04), 303–304 (2009)
11. Lian, F., Li, G., Chen, X., et al.: Chinese herbal medicine Tianqi reduces progression from impaired glucose tolerance to diabetes: a double-blind, randomized, placebo-controlled, multicenter trial. J. Clin. Endocrinol. Metab. **99**(02), 648–655 (2014)
12. Yanqin, S.: Clinical observation on preventing from community hypertension based on TCM health management. Clin. J. Chin. Med. **10**(04), 67 (2018)
13. Lin, B., Zhang, X., Zhang, Y., et al.: Design and implementation of Chinese medicine constitution recognition system. J. Chengdu Univ. Tradit. Chin. Med. **12**(39), 123–125 (2016)
14. Zhou, B., Lu, X., Hu, G., et al.: TCM health management system. In: 2010 Bioinformatics and Biomedicine, pp. 613–616. IEEE, Hong Kong (2010)

Early Warning and Response of Emerging Infectious Diseases with Hospitals as the Main Body

Hongchang An[✉]

China University of Labor Relations, Zengguang Road 45, Beijing, China

Abstract. The novel coronavirus pneumonia outbreak is the most alarming problem. Early warning is well done and the effect is good. Based on the analysis of the early-warning provisions of laws and regulations and the early-warning chain of emerging infectious diseases, it is considered that the graded early-warning and graded response of emerging infectious diseases with hospitals as the main body are of irreplaceable significance for emerging infectious diseases.

Keywords: Hospital · Emerging infectious diseases · Graded early-warning · Graded response

1 Introduction

Novel coronavirus pneumonia occurred in Wuhan, Hubei in December 2019. Later, there was infection among medical staff. After the early warning and systematic warning of the medical staff, the 3 National Health Protection Committee sent the group of experts to investigate. Until the third batch of senior expert group was sent to the academician Zhong Nanshan after the investigation in January 20, 2020, after the phenomenon of human transmission, the support of the CPC Central Committee and the State Council in Wuhan in January 2020. On the eve of the 23rd New Year's Eve, the city was closed down, and then Hubei Province and even the whole country adopted strict closed management measures. Even so, more than 80000 confirmed cases and more than 4000 deaths have been reported in China. Fortunately, it took us less than two months to basically control the epidemic. However, it is a pity that many countries have turned a deaf ear to the early warning issued by China and WHO. Now, the development trend is faster than that in the early stage of China, and there are nearly 5 million confirmed cases.

Since December 2019, China starting points novel coronavirus pneumonia situation in China and the world. First, China's Wuhan, then Hubei Province, and the whole country, now the world, especially Europe, the United States and Iran. Although it is not yet known where the real starting point of the epidemic is, it is undeniable that China and the world are not prepared to deal with this war without smoke. Bill Gates and other insightful people have been alerted and reminded. In the face of this war, both the central government and the local governments at all levels are more or less unsatisfactory. Even though there are many praises, on the whole, we are all losers.

© Springer Nature Singapore Pte Ltd. 2021
Y. Wang et al. (Eds.): DHA 2020, CCIS 1412, pp. 18–26, 2021.
https://doi.org/10.1007/978-981-16-3631-8_3

As far as China is concerned, the performance of the Hubei provincial and Wuhan municipal governments at first was very poor, but the good thing is that our country has a superior socialist system, the strong leadership of the Central Party and government and a solid industrial foundation, the concerted efforts of the people of the whole country, the attack of soldiers in white, the protection of police and traffic, and the selfless volunteers and community managers. The combination of traditional Chinese medicine and Western medicine, especially the advantages of traditional Chinese medicine, has taken scientific epidemic prevention and control measures and strategies in accordance with the law. The epidemic situation in China has been basically controlled, but the risk of foreign import is increasing, so we should not take it lightly, or we will lose all our previous achievements.

Novel coronavirus pneumonia in the prevention and control of the whole, the most puzzling is why Hubei and Wuhan have not yet issued an early warning of infectious diseases, but also make people most satisfied with the Wuhan city after the closure of the city's daily epidemic notification and early warning, which let all levels of government know, correct response, let people know what to do, actively cooperate with the government to deal with and do their own protection. Throughout the country and the world, the key to effective epidemic prevention and control is early warning.

2 Relevant Provisions on Early Warning

The controversy over the novel coronavirus pneumonia epidemic early warning is mainly concentrated on the authority of early warning. Some people find the excuse that Hubei Province and Wuhan city didn't issue early warning as soon as possible, because many laws and regulations have inconsistent provisions on the early warning authority. Let's take a look at the three most relevant laws and regulations on early warning.

2.1 Provisions of the Law on Prevention and Control of Infectious Diseases

Article 19 stipulates that the State shall establish an early warning system for infectious diseases. The administrative department of health under the State Council and the people's governments of provinces, autonomous regions and municipalities directly under the central government shall issue early warning of infectious diseases in a timely manner and make them known according to the situation on the basis of the prediction of the occurrence and epidemic trend of infectious diseases.

Article 20 stipulates that local people's governments and disease prevention and control institutions shall take corresponding preventive and control measures in accordance with the pre-warning plan for prevention and control of infectious diseases after receiving the early warning of infectious diseases issued by the health administrative department under the State Council or the people's governments of provinces, autonomous regions and municipalities directly under the central government.

Article 34 stipulates that the health administrative departments of the local people's governments at or above the county level shall promptly inform the disease prevention and control institutions and medical institutions within their respective administrative regions of the epidemic situation of infectious diseases and the relevant information of monitoring and early warning. The disease prevention and control institutions and medical institutions that have received the notification shall inform the relevant personnel of their own units in a timely manner.

Article 35 stipulates that the health administrative department under the State Council shall promptly inform other relevant departments under the State Council and the health administrative departments of the people's governments of provinces, autonomous regions and municipalities directly under the central government the epidemic situation of infectious diseases and relevant information on monitoring and early warning. The health administrative departments of the neighboring and relevant local people's governments shall timely inform each other of the epidemic situation of infectious diseases in their respective administrative regions and relevant information on monitoring and early warning.

Article 60 stipulates that the health administrative department of the State Council shall determine the prevention, control, treatment, monitoring, prediction, early warning, supervision and inspection of infectious diseases throughout the country in accordance with the epidemic trend of infectious diseases in conjunction with the relevant departments under the State Council. The central government will provide subsidies for the implementation of major infectious disease prevention and control projects in hard areas.

2.2 Provisions of Emergency Response Law

Article 2 stipulates that this Law shall be applicable to the prevention and emergency preparation, monitoring and early warning, emergency disposal and rescue, and post event recovery and reconstruction.

Article 15 stipulates that the government of the people's Republic of China shall cooperate and exchange with foreign governments and relevant international organizations in the prevention, monitoring and early warning of emergencies, emergency response and rescue, and post recovery and reconstruction.

Article 18 stipulates that the emergency plan shall specify the organization and command system and responsibilities of emergency management, prevention and early warning mechanism, handling procedures, emergency safeguard measures in accordance with the provisions of this law and other relevant laws and regulations and afterwards in accordance with the nature, characteristics and possible social hazards of emergencies restoration and reconstruction measures.

Article 36 stipulates that the State shall encourage and support teaching and scientific research institutions with corresponding conditions to cultivate specialized personnel for emergency management, and encourage and support teaching and research institutions and relevant enterprises to research and develop new technologies, new equipment and new tools for emergency prevention, monitoring, early warning, emergency response and rescue. The local people's governments at or above the county level shall timely summarize and analyze the hidden dangers and early warning information of emergencies, organize relevant departments, professional technicians, experts and scholars to hold consultations when necessary, and evaluate the possibility of the occurrence of the emergency and its possible impact; if it considers that a major or especially serious emergency may occur, it shall immediately report to the people's government at a higher level and inform the relevant departments of the people's government at a higher level, the local garrison and the people's governments of neighboring or related areas that may be endangered.

Article 42 stipulates that the State shall establish and improve the early warning system for emergencies. The early warning levels of natural disasters, accident disasters and public health events that can be early-warning can be divided into level 1, level 2, level 3 and level 4 according to the emergency degree, development trend and possible harm degree of emergencies, which are marked with red, orange, yellow and blue respectively, and level 1 is the highest level. The criteria for the classification of early warning levels shall be formulated by the State Council or the departments determined by the State Council.

Article 43 stipulates that when a natural disaster, accident disaster or public health event that can be forewarned is about to occur or the possibility of occurrence increases, the local people's governments at or above the county level shall issue an alarm at the corresponding level, and decide and announce the entry of the relevant area to the early warning in accordance with the relevant laws, administrative regulations and the limits of authority and procedures prescribed by the State Council. At the same time, it shall report to the people's government at the next higher level, and may report to the local garrison and the people's Government of the neighboring or related areas that may be endangered when necessary.

Article 44 stipulates that after issuing three or four level alarms and declaring the early warning period, local people's governments at or above the county level shall take the following measures according to the characteristics of the impending emergency and the possible harm: (1) Start the emergency plan; (2) Order relevant departments, professional institutions, monitoring network points and personnel with special responsibilities to collect and report relevant information in a timely manner, publicize channels to reflect the information of emergencies to the public, and strengthen the monitoring, forecasting and early warning of the occurrence and development of emergencies.

Article 45 stipulates that after issuing the first and second level alarms and declaring the early warning period, the local people's governments at or above the county level shall take one or more of the following measures in addition to the measures stipulated in article 44 of this law and according to the characteristics of the impending emergency and the possible harm it may cause: (1) Order the emergency rescue team and personnel with specific responsibilities to be on standby, and mobilize reserve personnel to prepare for emergency rescue and disposal work; (2) Mobilize materials, equipment and tools needed for emergency rescue, prepare emergency facilities and shelters, and ensure that they are in good condition and can be put into normal use at any time.

Article 47 stipulates that the people's government that issues an emergency warning shall timely adjust the warning level and issue it again in accordance with the development of the situation and in accordance with relevant provisions. If it is proved by facts that an emergency is unlikely to occur or the danger has been removed, the people's government that issued the alarm shall immediately announce the cancellation of the alarm, terminate the early warning period and lift the relevant measures already taken.

Article 63 stipulates that if a local people's government at any level or a relevant department of a people's government at or above the county level violates the provisions of this Law and fails to perform its statutory duties, it shall be ordered by its superior administrative organ or supervisory organ to make corrections; in case of any of the following circumstances, the directly responsible person in charge and other directly responsible persons shall be punished according to the circumstances: (1) Failure to take preventive measures as required, resulting in an emergency, or failure to take necessary preventive measures, leading to the occurrence of secondary or derivative events; (2) Late report, false report, concealment or omission of information related to emergencies, or reporting, submitting or publishing false information, resulting in consequences; (3) Failing to timely issue an emergency warning or take measures in the early warning period as required, resulting in damage.

2.3 Provisions of Regulations on Public Health Emergencies

Article 7 stipulates that the State encourages and supports international exchanges and cooperation in technologies related to emergency monitoring, early warning and response handling.

Article 11 stipulates that the national emergency plan shall include the following main contents: (1) Composition of emergency response headquarters and responsibilities of relevant departments; (2) Emergency monitoring and early warning.

Article 14 stipulates that the State shall establish a unified emergency prevention and control system. Local people's governments at or above the county level shall establish and improve emergency monitoring and early warning systems. The health administrative departments of the people's governments at or above the county level shall designate institutions to be responsible for the daily monitoring of emergencies and ensure the normal operation of the monitoring and early warning system.

Article 15 stipulates that the monitoring and early warning work shall formulate monitoring plans, scientifically analyze and comprehensively evaluate the monitoring data according to the categories of emergencies. Potential hidden dangers discovered in the early stage and possible emergencies shall be reported in a timely manner in accordance with the reporting procedures and time limit stipulated in these regulations. Comprehensive analysis of the above-mentioned laws and regulations shows that there is no obvious conflict in the expression about early warning. The reasons for the problems lie in the fact that the relevant personnel do not know the law or think the law is illegal to himself, and the other is that they are indifferent to the people's life safety and health.

Comprehensive analysis of the above-mentioned laws and regulations shows that there is no obvious conflict in the expression about early warning. The reasons for the problems lie in the fact that the relevant personnel do not know the law or think the law is illegal to himself, and the other is that they are indifferent to the people's life safety and health.

3 Early Warning Chain of Emerging Infectious Diseases

According to the development history of new major infectious diseases and the early warning methods of each link, the early warning chain of new major infectious diseases is shown in Fig. 1.

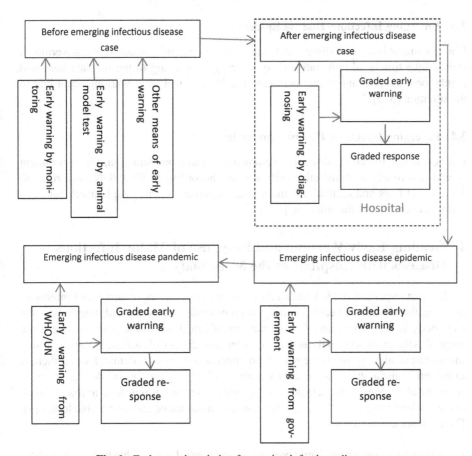

Fig. 1. Early warning chain of emerging infectious diseases.

3.1 Before Emerging Infectious Disease Case

According to the relevant literature, we can use early warning methods such as monitoring and animal experimental model warning before the emergence of new major infectious diseases [1]. Professor Jing Jun of Tsinghua University has also proposed a multi-source early warning system for enterprise participation, research institution participation, public participation, reporting hospital infection and the charm of small data.

3.2 After Emerging Infectious Disease Case

After the emergence of new major infectious diseases, it should be the diagnosis and early warning of hospitals as the main body [2]. The Eighth People's Hospital of Guangzhou has achieved good results in grading early warning and response from 2001 to 2003, which is a good experience.

3.3 Emerging Infectious Disease Epidemic

If a new major infectious disease develops into an epidemic situation, the government should take timely administrative early warning. According to the relevant laws and regulations, the relevant government can take hierarchical early warning according to the situation [3–5].

3.4 Emerging Infectious Disease Pandemic

If a new major infectious disease develops into a pandemic situation, the government should take timely administrative early warning according to WHO/UN. According to the relevant laws and regulations, the relevant government can take hierarchical early warning according to the situation [6–8].

4 Grading Early Warning and Response of Major Infectious Diseases with Hospitals as the Main Body

As the most important and key link in the chain of early warning of new major infectious diseases, the hierarchical early warning and hierarchical response with hospitals as the main body is very important. A large number of infectious diseases tell us that if the hospital as the main body of the new major infectious disease classification early warning and hierarchical response, there will be no infectious disease epidemic. Even if there is an epidemic, the administrative early warning will be very timely, and do a good job in hierarchical response, and achieve good results, otherwise it will lead to the outbreak of the epidemic and pandemic, and then cause immeasurable and irreparable losses [9]. The contents are as follows:

1) A leading group for epidemic prevention and control was established, with the hospital leaders as the group leader and the director of the nursing department participating. The team was fully responsible for the prevention and control of the hospital, and regularly summarized the situation. The leaders of the nursing department adjusted the focus of nursing work according to the situation of the hospital, and formulated new measures according to the new situation In order to ensure the allocation of human resources, the nursing work will not be disordered because of emergencies.

2) The operational efficiency of the management system of emergency epidemic management system is not only reflected in the responsiveness to emergencies, but also in the predictability and prevention plan for emergencies. When the hospital receives the epidemic situation, it shall immediately call a meeting to review the original emergency response plan of the system, revise the unsuitable part, and supplement and formulate the specific contents on the prevention and control of infectious diseases. The plan includes the nursing plan for dealing with a large number of infectious patients in common and major epidemic situations, formulating regional treatment management plan, and dividing special areas for diagnosis and treatment, inspection, treatment and nursing of epidemic patients. And select and equip doctors and nurses with relatively fixed personnel, and provide a variety of medical care equipment and equipment and nursing supplies.

3) According to the degree of harm, emergency degree and development trend of infectious diseases, the early warning level is divided into four levels, and different early warning response is divided according to the epidemic level. ① Level IV early warning: in case of suspected cases within the scope of the city or the epidemic situation in neighboring cities posing a direct threat to the city, level IV emergency response shall be initiated. ② Level III early warning: when scattered clinical diagnosis cases, laboratory confirmed cases or imported cases occur within the city, level III emergency response shall be started, and further measures shall be taken on the basis of implementing level IV emergency response. ③ Grade II early warning: in case of single point or multi-point aggregation cases in the city, the level II emergency response shall be started. ④ Grade I early warning: for a particularly serious group of unexplained diseases with strong infectivity and a tendency to spread, level I early warning and emergency response will be initiated.

4) The ratio of patients with mild infectious diseases to nursing staff is 1:0.4, the ratio of patients with severe infectious diseases to nursing staff is 1:0.8-1, the ratio of patients with mild infectious diseases to nursing staff is 1:0.8-1, and the ratio of patients with mild SARS to nursing staff is 1:0.8- The ratio of severe SARS patients to nursing staff was 1:3-10.

5   Conclusions

Through the novel coronavirus pneumonia case, let us rethink and focus on early warning, and think that early warning plays a very important role in the prevention and treatment of new major infectious diseases [10]. Especially the hospital based grading warning and grading response is riding on the link between the preceding and the following, and we should attach great importance to it. Units at all levels should refer to the hospital to set up their own three to four levels of early warning response mechanism, so as to achieve early detection, early warning, early report, early isolation and early treatment.

Acknowledgments. This paper is supported by the National Natural Science Foundation of China (NSFC) "social media health knowledge discovery and personalized diagnosis and treatment method research" (project approval number: 71572013) and general project of China Institute of labor relations (20xyjs023).

References

1. Gong, L., Zhang, J., Chen, G., et al.: A review on the epidemic and early identification and early warning of emerging infectious diseases. Anhui J. Prevent. Med. (02), 117–121, 132 (2015).
2. Lin, M., Wang, X., Liang, D.: Progress in application of symptom monitoring in early warning of emerging infectious diseases and outbreaks Chin. J. Prevent. Med. (07), 659–664 (2015)
3. Chen, L., Wang, Y., Zhang, B.: Research on diagnosis and differential diagnosis early warning system of emerging infectious diseases. Infect. Disease Inf. (4), 243–245 (2008)
4. Wang, H., Zhou, X.: Early warning strategies for emerging and recurring infectious diseases. Chin. J. Infect. Diseases (01), 60–62 (2010)

5. Tian, G., Gao, Z.: Clinical status and its associated early warning per emerging infectious respiratory disease in China. Chin. Med. J. **127**(17), 3043–3045 (2014)
6. Rashid, A., Chotani, A.L.: To enhance the technical capabilities in establishing an early warning system for emerging infectious diseases. Eur. J. Publ. Health **14**(4s), 91 (2002)
7. Cibrelus, L., Noeel, V., Emmanuelli, J., et al.: Experience of a collaboration between epidemiologists and clinicians facing an emerging infectious disease health alert. Medecine et Maladies Infectieuses **37**(3s), S242–S250 (2007)
8. Nakajima, H.: Emerging infectious disease: global response, global alert. Health the Millions **23**(2), 19 (1997)
9. Zeng, F., Li, A., Guan, Y.: Effect analysis of the application of hierarchical early warning operation mode in the epidemic situation of major infectious diseases. Mod. Clin. Nurs. **5**(04), 67–69 (2006)
10. Zhai, Y., et al.: From isolation to coordination: how can telemedicine help combat the Covid-19 outbreak? MedRxiv (2020)

Exploring Patients' AI Adoption Intention in the Context of Healthcare

Yiwei Zhu and Shiwei Sun[✉]

School of Economics and Management, Beijing Institute of Technology, Beijing 100081, China
shiweisun@bit.edu.cn

Abstract. Artificial intelligence (AI) produces positive effects on the productivity and efficiency for organizations and is widely adopted in various contexts. Although individuals' adoption of new technology has been studied widely, very few studies has been devoted to the adoption of AI in the context of healthcare. Based on technology adoption related theories, the study explains how the proposed factors impact patients' trust toward AI technology and in turn their adoption attention. Using 304 patients' sample, we built the conceptual model and conclude that trust toward AI technology, perceived ease of use, relative advantage, and perceived risk in the healthcare background significantly affect AI adoption intention. Our study thus extends the understanding of AI use in the healthcare industry.

Keywords: AI adoption intention · Healthcare industry · Main factors

1 Introduction

According to the report, approximate 12 million adults each year in the U.S seeking outpatient medical care are misdiagnosed (Winters et al. 2012). Researchers conclude half of these misdiagnosis cases are caused more severe harms due to the lack of effective treatment (Winters et al. 2012). The traditional healthcare industry faces numerous challenges related to the nature of healthcare services that should be provided in high quality and efficiency. Prior research has shown that healthcare services can be enhanced and improved through the implementation of technology innovations (Wamba 2012; Yao et al. 2012). The rapid development of automatic control technology, robotics, big data analytics, artificial intelligence (AI) technologies is moving forward the revolution of healthcare industry (Wang et al. 2018, 2019). Meanwhile, the emergence of Industry 4.0 is expected to attract worldwide attention, indicating that the fourth technological revolution has come. With the evolution and popularity of the Internet, AI techniques are gradually rising and developing. In addition, AI is beginning to be adopted in various areas such as the catering services in the hospitality industry (Li et al. 2019). In the healthcare industry, the applications of AI range from medical records and prevention to intelligence diagnosis and treatment. Among them, "AI plus auxiliary diagnosis" including deep learning and neural networks can improve the accuracy of auxiliary diagnosis (Zhang et al. 2019a).

© Springer Nature Singapore Pte Ltd. 2021
Y. Wang et al. (Eds.): DHA 2020, CCIS 1412, pp. 27–39, 2021.
https://doi.org/10.1007/978-981-16-3631-8_4

To understand how AI provides better medical services for patients, it is necessary to figure out the mechanisms by which the related factors impact patients' acceptance. Past literature indicates that perceived ease of use, perceived usefulness and trust toward technologies or platforms have positive impact on use intention (Genfen et al. 2003; Polites and Karahanna 2012). However, there is no empirical study to explore how these antecedents affect AI adoption intention in the context of healthcare. Similarly, while prior research indicates that perceived privacy risk and fear of technological advances affect users' adoption intention toward some specific technologies or platforms (Hart 2006; Brown and Venkatesh 2005), the exact mechanism by which these factors may impact AI adoption intention in healthcare has not been fully studied.

There is research providing insights into who adopts new things and why (Liao and Cheung 2001). In our research context, intention-based theories such as the theory of planned behavior (TPB) (Ajzen 1991), the technology acceptance model (TAM) (Davis 1989) and the theory of reasoned action (TRA) (Fishbein and Ajzen 1975) can be taken for model building in our study.

In the following section we begin with the theoretical background, reviewing and summarizing prior work on the new technology adoption intention, the definition of artificial intelligence and its applications in the healthcare. Following that, our research hypotheses and the research model are present. The paper then give the details of our methodology. Finally, the results of empirical tests are discussed, we further discussed the significance of our findings and then concluded theoretical and practical implications.

2 Theoretical Background

2.1 Artificial Intelligence in Healthcare

Researchers predicted that most of clinician, will be using AI technology for a better medical treatment in the future (Topol 2019). For example, it will become clear that AI technologies are able to equal or even surpass humans to complete simple or repetitive tasks. For example, electronic medical record documentation can be automated by AI system to a large degree. Besides, these systems may be even able to undertake the bulk of the unpleasant and some dirty work in the context of healthcare (Fogel and Kvedar 2018).

Most AI studies in healthcare realm are focusing on technical innovation and clinical results. However, they ignore the ethical challenges that are involved in the interaction between AI system and users. Specifically, in the context of healthcare, many real-world issues must be assessed before the implementation phase. These challenges may include to what extent patients or the public's concerns to accept AI and how to protect patients' privacy and the confidential medical record if AI is truly adopted in practice. Therefore, understanding the antecedents that affect public acceptance and adoption intention of AI in healthcare will help minimize patients' concerns and thus help government and hospitals, make proper regulations to effectively use AI.

2.2 Factors Influencing AI Adoption

In our research, followed by Davis (1989)'s study, we defined perceived ease of use of AI technology as the effort degree to using the new technology. Followed by Polites and

Karahnna (2012)'s research, we use relative advantage instead of perceived usefulness and defined relative advantage as the extent that patients believe AI technology in the healthcare background will help their treatment better compared to the current treatment patterns.

The negative sides are likely to affect patients accept AI. The risks and worries such as information disclosure perceived by patients will significantly influence their acceptance intention. Taken and modified from Hart (2006)'s research, we defined perceived risk as "perceived risk of opportunism behavior associated with the disclosure of personal privacy information if patients accept AI technology in the context of healthcare". Fear of technological advances, followed by Venkatesh and Brown (2001)'s research, we defined it as "the rapidly changing technology is related to fear of apprehension and obsolescence to what extent in the context of healthcare" to better adapt to our research background. Trust has been conceptualized by previous study in a variety of ways, and researchers have acknowledged the confusion in the field long before. Adapted from Gefen (2000)'s study, we defined trust toward AI technology as "Willingness to depend AI technology and trust the accuracy of specific prediction algorithms in the context of healthcare".

We conceptualize and operationalize the AI adoption intention construct as "the extent to which the patients would consent to have their private health information analyzed by AI technology and making further treatment plan" or an opt-in behavioral intention (Ajzen 1991; Davis et al. 1989) to adapt our healthcare research background.

3 Model and Hypothesis Development

With the development of AI technologies, the potential users to embrace these technologies depend largely on antecedents such as perceived risk, perceived usefulness of technology, users' perceived ease of use, trust etc. Many technology adoption models have been used to explain the acceptance and adoption process of an emerging technology and evaluate to what extent these factors can affect users' acceptance intention (Holden and Karsh 2010). Figure 1 depicts our research model.

3.1 The Impact of Relative Advantage and Perceived Ease of Use

Our objective was to understand patients' acceptance of AI in healthcare. As most regions do not have access to AI technologies and AI in healthcare is not mature currently, AI is proposed as a replacement or just assistant of doctors, followed by Polites and Karahnna (2012)'s research, we use relative advantage instead of perceived usefulness. As suggested by Cao et al.'s (2020) study, perceived ease of use is selected to predict AI adoption intention. AI adoption intention is our main interest in this study. We thus proposed the following hypothesis:

H1: Relative advantage positively influences the public's AI adoption intention in the context of healthcare.
H2a: Perceived ease of use positively influences the public's AI adoption intention in the context of healthcare.

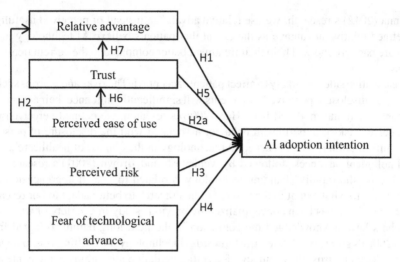

Fig. 1. Conceptual model

H2b: Perceived ease of use positively influences the public's perception of the AI relative advantage in the context of healthcare.

3.2 The Impact of Perceived Risk and Fear of Technological Advance

The theory of planned behavior (TPB) aims to interpret how people change their behavior patterns (Ajzen 1991). Among participants in Australia and Israel, Jarvenpaa et al. (1999) found that perceived risk and intention to buy have a consistent negative correlation. In the background of online auction seller's community, Pavlou and Gefen (2004) found a negative correlation between perceived risk and intention to transact. In Brown and Venkatsh (2005)'s study, they classified the antecedents of behavioral intention into three major classes based on TPB: attitudinal beliefs, normative beliefs, and control beliefs. In these three major classes, control beliefs include variables such as fear of technological advance and cost, which will discourage users' behavioral intention. In our study, we introduced the fear of technological advances into our model to study how it can affect the patient's AI adoption intention. In the view of patients, some of them may consider technological progress good, but resistance subconsciously because they fear that whether the technology is reliable and they need to confirm its suitability, thus reducing their adoption intention of AI. Thus, in the early stage of AI technological adoption and development in the context of healthcare, patients will experience fear of technological advance, the greater the fear of technological advance, the lower the AI adoption intention of patients. Thus, we proposed the following hypothesis:

H3: Perceived risk negatively affects the public's AI adoption intention in the context of healthcare.
H4: Fear of technological advance negatively affects the public's AI adoption intention in the context of healthcare.

3.3   The Mediation Role of Trust

Many studies have suggested that behavioral intention could be directly influenced by the trust. Trust reduces people's perceived uncertainty and provides a sense of satisfaction. It also allows people to subjectively rule out undesirable outcomes. In the context of healthcare, trust toward AI technology is crucial, only when AI technology such as tumor prediction algorithm and the next treatment plan can be trusted will the patients willing to accept AI technology and generate adoption intention. In this way, trust increases patients' or potential users' AI adoption intention and thus encourages them to adopt AI technology in healthcare. Therefore, the following hypothesis is presented:

H5: Trust toward AI technology positively affects the public's AI adoption intention in the context of healthcare.

In online transactions and e-commerce, perceived ease of use has been studied to have a positive impact on trust (Wu and Chen 2005). Through the perception that AI technologies are being invested, trust should be increased by perceived ease of use, which signals a commitment to the ease of use. With more efforts are placed on researching AI technologies, the application of AI in healthcare are becoming more usable and controllable. It is easy to conclude that both the researchers AI technologies will be much easier to use with the advancement of technical optimization. This will boost patients' trust towards AI. Therefore, a direct correlation between perceived ease of use and trust is expected as follow:

H6: Perceived ease of use positively affects the public's trust toward AI technology in the context of healthcare.

Amin et al. (2014) introduced trust as a mediation variable into model, a total of 302 questionnaires were collected, research indicated that trust mediate the relationship between perceived usefulness and mobile user satisfaction. Only when an AI technology can be trusted will the patients be able to reduce their resistance. Compared with traditional medical service, if an AI technology has a low capability and cannot serve patients better by improving treatment accuracy, patients will feel difficult to get the advantage of AI. Trust establishes the availability and credibility of AI technology to provide efficient treatment. According to trust theory, patients may suffer a loss from AI prediction or treatment when other parts does not behave as expected. It means that patients' perception of the AI relative advantage will be positively influenced by trust toward AI technology. Hence, we posit the following hypotheses:

H7: Trust toward AI technology positively affects the public's perception of the AI relative advantage in the context of healthcare.

4 Methodology

4.1 Sampling

The target participants are patients seeking medical service. Survey approach is the best method for our data collection work. The electronic questionnaire was published on the third-party data collection website (Wjx.cn), which is the largest and most famous data collection service provider in China. A total of 319 questionnaires were returned. After screening out invalid and incomplete responses, yielding final 304 usable responses for analysis, with a recovery rate of 95.30%. Considering the research context, the sample of this study was taken from the general patients who have their own knowledge and understanding of AI in different city of China (Zhang et al. 2019b). Before our respondents filled out the questionnaire, we explain the definition of AI technologies and describe what AI technologies can do in the context of healthcare.

4.2 Instrument Development

The 7 constructs in the research model were measured using 24 items. Existing scales were adapted for the context of this study. Items in English were back translated into Chinese carefully and checked. All items were measured on seven-point Likert scale ranging from "strongly disagree = 1" to "strongly agree = 7".

Perceived risk. Three items were adapted from prior studies (Hart 2006) and modified to fit the healthcare context. Sample items included: "I believe my electronic personal health information is at risk of being sold to third parties". Trust. A four-item scale developed by Genfen et al. (2003) was used to measure patient's AI adoption intention in the context of healthcare. Sample question included: "I believe that the use of AI treatment in hospitals is for patients". Relative advantage. Three items were taken from Polites and Karahanna (2012) and modified to fit the study's healthcare context. For example, respondents were asked if they agreed that "Compared with traditional treatment, using AI to treat patients in healthcare, would increase the accuracy of diagnosis". Perceived ease of use. Two items were adapted from Polites and Karahanna (2012). Sample questions included: "I think AI easy to use for treating patients in hospitals". Fears of technological advances. Three items were taken from Brown and Venkatesh (2005) and modified to fit the healthcare context. Sample items included: "I am worried about the rapid advances in AI". AI adoption intention. Three items were taken from Angst and Agarwal (2009) with modified to fit our study context. Sample questions included: "I would like to use AI technology to treat myself".

5 Data Analysis and Results

5.1 Descriptive Statistical Analysis

Among 304 participants, to ensure the reliability of the results, all of the respondents were over 18 years old, the largest group of patients is aged from 18–30 (69.4%). Beyond that, participants older than 50 years old are about 2.3%. Regarding education, 12.2% of the response group report education of high school degree or lower, bachelor's degrees accounted for 56.9%, and 30.9% of them report education of master's degree or higher. The questionnaire also covers a variety of occupations, including students (37.5%), specialist (30.9%), sales service (3.9%), technical post (19.4%), and others (8.3%). In general, the sample is representative for further analysis.

5.2 Measurement Validity and Reliability

We used AMOS 23.0 and SPSS 25 to examine the structural validity of the scale. Reliability and validity results were showed in Table 1. The coefficient of Cronbach's alpha (α) is greater than 0.791, exceeding the recommended cutoff of 0.7 (Nunnaly 1978), showing that the reliability of questionnaires is good. Composite reliability scores for the final reflectively measured scaled ranged from 0.821 to 0.905, and all were above the standard of 0.7. For convergent validity, the AVE has to exceed 0.5 (Fornell and Larcker 1981), indicating that the AVE of the seven factors in the model was up to scratch, manifesting that the questionnaire has good validity.

Table 1. Construct reliability, CR and AVE

Construct	Code	Mean	S.D	Alpha	CR	AVE
Relative advantage	RA	4.8838	1.36742	0.879	0.879	0.709
Perceived ease of use	PEOU	5.0313	1.41766	0.860	0.8604	0.755
Perceived risk	PR	5.3279	1.48296	0.905	0.905	0.761
Fear of technological advances	FTA	3.7873	1.65488	0.891	0.893	0.736
Trust	TRU	4.7286	1.36808	0.891	0.886	0.661
AI adoption intention	AIAI	4.6535	1.45807	0.896	0.899	0.747

Table 2 shows the correlations among variables. Diagonal entries list the square root of AVE extracted for the corresponding structure. If the square root of each AVE exceeds the correlation between this construct and all other conceptually similar constructs in this research, discriminant validity can be ensured (MacKenzie et al. 2011). As the table shows, all the constructs satisfy the above criteria. This finding suggests that convergent and discriminant validity were warranted, and that our measurements were adequate psychometrically.

5.3 Structural Equation Modeling Analysis

In our research, we use Amos 23.0 to assess the structural equation model (SEM). Our result showed that no variables were single-item variables, and our model include observed variables, latent variables, and the interaction between different variables. We use SEM to analyze data instead of traditional regression analysis. The data results obtained by the model are a 1.698 chi-square degree of freedom ratio, GFI = 0.930, NFI = 0.949, CFI = 0.978, RMSEA = 0.048 TLI = 0.973, based on the model fitting degree

Table 2. Correlations

Construct	RA	PEOU	PR	FTA	PC	TRU	AIAI
RA							
PEOU	0.597						
PR	0.293	0.223					
FTA	0.306	0.301	0.696				
PC	0.225	0.301	0.699	0.78			
TRU	0.259	0.214	0.060	0.015	0.018		
AIAI	0.125	0.074	0.602	0.609	0.597	−0.055	

test, which are all up to the standard of good fitting degree. The model explains 54% of the variance in patients' AI adoption intention in healthcare. Table 3 shows there are no significant deviation between our model and the real data.

Table 3. Model results

Model	χ^2/df	GFI	CFI	NFI	TLI	RMSEA
Criteria	≤ 3	≥ 0.90	≥ 0.90	≥ 0.90	≥ 0.90	≤ 0.08
Final	1.691	0.929	0.978	0.949	0.973	0.048

The hypothesis we proposed before has been tested in Table 4. In the context of healthcare, the relative advantage is related to AI adoption intention positively ($\beta = 0.360$, $p < 0.05$), supporting H1. PEOU is positively associated with relative advantage ($\beta = 0.753$, $p < 0.001$), but not significantly correlated with AI adoption intention ($\beta = 0.133$, $p > 0.05$), supporting H2b but not H2a. The perceived risk reduces AI adoption intention ($\beta = -0.158$, $p < 0.01$), H3 was supported. Fear of technological advantage negatively related to AI adoption intention but not statistically significant ($\beta = -0.053$, $p > 0.5$), H4 is rejected. Trust toward AI technology positively affects AI adoption intention ($\beta = 0.323$, $p < 0.001$), supporting H5. PEOU affects trust toward AI technology positively ($\beta = 0.799$, $p < 0.001$), and trust toward AI technology positively affect relative advantage ($\beta = 0.182$, $p < 0.05$), indicating H6 and H7 are supported.

To estimate whether the antecedents of trust and PEOU affect AI adoption intention indirectly, we conducted bootstrapping tests (Preacher and Hayes 2008). Table 5 demonstrated that the relationships between PEOU and AIAI were mediated by relative advantage and trust toward AI technology. Since for the indirect effects, zero was contained in the 95% percentile-based confidence intervals, the relationships between trust and AIAI were not mediated by relative advantage.

Table 4. The results of path analysis

Equilibrium correlations	Standardized estimate (β)	P value	C.R
RA → AIAI	0.360	0.025	2.248
PEOU → AIAI	0.133	0.434	0.782
PEOU → RA	0.753	0.000	8.344
PR → AIAI	−0.158	0.003	−2.995
FTA → AIAI	−0.053	0.275	−1.092
TRU → AIAI	0.323	0.000	3.320
PEOU → TRU	0.799	0.000	12.503
TRU → RA	0.182	0.027	2.209

Table 5. Mediation mechanism

Indirect paths	Point estimate	Bootstrapping	
		Percentile 95% CI	
		Lower	Upper
Trust → AIAI	0.066	−0.004	0.188
PEOU → RA	0.146	0.003	0.324
PEOU → AIAI	0.581	0.175	0.978

5.4 Common Method Bias

There is a possibility for common method bias as our data were self-reported data. Followed by Podsakoff and Organ (1986), we asking the respondent to get the information of AI function from minutes of information seeking or documentation instead of evaluate the function of AI in the context of healthcare according to individual experience. Moreover, statistical analyses were conducted to estimate the common method bias. A Harmon one-factor test (Podsakoff and Organ 1986) was used on the seven conceptually key variables in our theoretical model including perceived ease of use, perceived risk, relative advantage, fear of technological advances, trust and AI adoption intention. Test results showed that seven variables are present and the most covariance explained by one variable is 34.74%, suggesting that there are no signs for common method bias influence.

6 Discussion and Conclusions

The structural equation model is used in our study to explore the antecedents of patients' AI adoption intention in the context of healthcare based on TAM, DFT, and TPB. In the context of healthcare, the empirical results show that relative advantage, perceived risk, and trust toward AI technology all directly affect AI adoption intention and PEOU through trust toward AI adoption intention and relative advantage indirectly affect AI adoption intention. Among them, relative advantage has the largest direct impact on AI adoption intention.

6.1 Theoretical and Practical Implications

Healthcare requires advanced technologies in this competitive marketing environment, offering accurate and efficient treatment. The study results in the above synopsis conductive to the new healthcare technologies acceptance and adoption literature in several ways. First, our present study uses TAM as the theoretical foundation and developed research models in the context of healthcare to explore the antecedents of patients' AI adoption intention. While TAM has been widely studied in online shopping and new systems acceptance in enterprises, inadequate scholarly attention has been drawn to new technologies acceptance and adoption in the context of healthcare, in our research, we applied the TAM to the healthcare context, expanded the application fields of TAM. The demand patterns from patients in the healthcare background are increasingly challenging, hospitals should consider not merely how to treat patients, but also to improve the accuracy and efficiency of treatment, with AI technologies are able to help achieve this goal. Second, for hospitals to accept AI technologies, they must start with understand the main factors that affect the patient's adoption intention. Thus, it is significant to verify the antecedents of AI adoption intention in the context of healthcare as early as possible for hospitals to be able to provide patients better service and treatment. This research's findings confirm that when patients have higher trust toward AI technology and when AI treatment has a higher relative advantage than doctor's treatment, patients are likely to have higher AI adoption intentions. As for the perceived ease of use, it affects AI adoption intention indirectly through relative advantage and trust toward AI technology. Besides, the perceived risk of AI technology will decrease patients' AI adoption intention. This result is further confirmed the universality of TAM.

As for practical implications, our study results indicate some additional hospitals managerial practices in the Chinese healthcare industry. Patients' AI adoption intention should be activated through relative advantage and trust toward AI technology. In order to introduce AI technology better and faster in the healthcare industry, it should build patients' trust toward AI technology further, increase AI technology's perceived ease of use and relative advantage. Moreover, when a hospital is about to adopt AI technology, the staff in the hospital should try to decrease patient's perceived risk toward AI technology though some measures such as promote the knowledge of AI technology to eliminate the patient's vigilance. To achieve these objectives, first, during the development of medical AI technology, algorithm engineers can try to increase the accuracy of the prediction algorithm so that the patients' perceived ease of use toward AI technology and the relative advantage of AI technology in the context of healthcare can be improved. Second, after the introduction of AI technology, related technologist can further improve AI technology according to the judgement accuracy and treatment effect, healthcare workers can learn basic knowledge of AI technology and explain how it works to the patients, thus reducing the patients' perceived risk toward AI technology.

6.2 Limitations and Suggestions for Future Research

This research contains some limitations that provide directions for future study. First, as the technology of AI is not mature in the healthcare industry, we used AI adoption intention as the outcome. We provide only empirical evidence of AI adoption intention in the healthcare industry. We haven't traced the actual adoption behavior of patients. Hence, the results are limited for a continuing discussion of actual AI adoption behavior in the healthcare industry.

Second, the key points of this paper are on the antecedents of AI adoption intention in the context of healthcare, we concentrate on several independent variables and our model explains 54% of the variance in patients' AI adoption intention in the healthcare industry. The results show that there exist other antecedents that will affect AI adoption intentions. Future research can further introduce more factors into our model.

Third, the generalizability of our findings is limited, as the data were collected from China. Culture setting may affect our conclusion. Due to the culture difference, people in other countries may have different attitudes toward AI technology in the context of healthcare. Therefore, future studies are called to include samples from different nations to further validate the results.

References

Ajzen, I.: The theory of planned behaviour is alive and well, and not ready to retire: a commentary on sniehotta, presseau, and araújo-soares. Health Psychol. Rev. **9**(2), 1–7 (2014)

Ajzen, I.: The theory of planned behavior. Org. Behav. Hum. Decis. Process. **50**(2), 179–211 (1991)

Allen, B., Jr., Seltzer, S.E., Langlotz, C.P., et al.: A road map for translational research on artificial intelligence in medical imaging: from the 2018 National Institutes of Health/RSNA/ACR/The Academy Workshop. J. Am. Coll. Radiol. **16**(9), 1179–1189 (2019)

Amin, M., Rezaei, S., Abolghasemi, M.: User satisfaction with mobile websites: the impact of perceived usefulness (PU), perceived ease of use (PEOU) and trust. Nankai Bus. Rev. Int. **5**(3), 258–274 (2014)

Brown, S.A., Venkatesh, V.: Model of adoption of technology in households: a baseline model test and extension incorporating household life cycle. MIS Q. **29**(3), 399–426 (2005)

Cao, D., Tao, H., Wang, Y., Tarhini, A., Xia, S.: Acceptance of automation manufacturing technology in China: an examination of perceived norm and organizational efficacy. Prod. Plan. Control **31**(8), 660–672 (2020)

David, W., Zaki, H.: Developing an artificial intelligence-enabled health care practice: rewiring health care professions for better care. J. Med. Imaging Radiat. Sci. **50**(4), S8–S14 (2019)

Davis, F.D., Warshaw, P.R.: What do intention scales measure? J. Gen. Psychol. **119**(4), 391–407 (1992)

Davis, F.D., Bagozzi, R.P., Warshaw, P.R.: User acceptance of computer technology: a comparison of two theoretical models. Manag. Sci. **35**(8), 982–1003 (1989)

Davis, F.D.: Perceived usefulness, perceived ease of use, and user acceptance of information technology. MIS Q. **13**(3), 319–340 (1989)

Dou, K., Yu, P., Deng, N., Liu, F., Duan, H.: Patients' acceptance of smartphone health technology for chronic disease management: a theoretical model and empirical test. Jmir Mhealth Uhealth **5**(12), e177 (2017)

Esteva, A., Kuprel, B., Novoa, R.A., Ko, J., Swetter, S.M., Blau, H.M., et al.: Dermatologist-level classification of skin cancer with deep neural networks. Nature **542**(7639), 115–118 (2017)

Fishbein, M., Ajzen, I.: Belief, Attitude, Intention and Behavior an Introduction to Theory and Research. Addison-Wesley, Reading (1975)

Fogel, A.L., Kvedar, J.C.: Artificial intelligence powers digital medicine. NPJ Digit. Med. **1**(1), 5 (2018)

Fornell, C., Larcker, D.F.: Evaluating structural equation models with unobservable variables and measurement error. J. Mark. Res. **18**(1), 39–50 (1981)

Gao, B., Huang, L.: Understanding interactive user behavior in smart media content service: an integration of TAM and smart service belief factors. Heliyon **5**(12), e02983 (2019)

Gefen, D., Straub, K.D.W.: Trust and TAM in online shopping: an integrated model. MIS Q. **27**(1), 51–90 (2003)

Gefen, D.: E-commerce: the role of familiarity and trust. Omega **28**(6), 725–737 (2000)

Hart, D.P.: An extended privacy calculus model for e-commerce transactions. Inf. Syst. Res. **17**(1), 61–80 (2006)

Holden, R.J., Karsh, B.T.: The technology acceptance model: its past and its future in health care. J. Biomed. Inform. **43**(1), 159–172 (2010)

Jarvenpaa, S.L., Tractinsky, N., Saarinen, L.: Consumer trust in an internet store: a cross-cultural validation. J. Comput. Mediat. Commun. **5**(2) (1999)

Kerlinger F.: Foundations of Behavioral Research. Holt, Rinehart and Mnston, New York (1984)

Kim, J., Park, H.A.: Development of a health information technology acceptance model using consumers' health behavior intention. J. Med. Internet Res. **14**(5), e133 (2012)

Lee, Y., Kozar, K.A., Larsen, K.R.T.: The technology acceptance model: past, present, and future. Commun. Assoc. Inf. Syst. **12**(50), 752–780 (2003)

Li, J., Bonn, M.A., Ye, B.H.: Hotel employee's artificial intelligence and robotics awareness and its impact on turnover intention: the moderating roles of perceived organizational support and competitive psychological climate. Tour. Manag. **73**, 172–181 (2019)

Mackenzie, S.B., Podsakoff, P.M., Podsakoff, N.P.: Construct measurement and validation procedures in MIS and behavioral research: integrating new and existing techniques. MIS Q. **35**(2), 293–334 (2011)

Pavlou, P.A., Gefen, D.: Building effective online marketplaces with institution-based trust. Inf. Syst. Res. **15**(1), 37–59 (2004)

Podsakoff, P.M.: Self-reports in organizational research: problems and prospects. J. Manag. **12**(4), 531–544 (1986)

Polites, G.L., Karahanna, E.: Shackled to the status quo: the inhibiting effects of incumbent system habit, switching costs, and inertia on new system acceptance. MIS Q. **36**(1), 21–42 (2012)

Preacher, K.J., Hayes, A.F.: Asymptotic and resampling strategies for assessing and comparing indirect effects in multiple mediator models. Behav. Res. Methods **40**(3), 879–891 (2008)

Topol, E.J.: High-performance medicine: the convergence of human and artificial intelligence. Nat. Med. **25**(1), 44 (2019)

Venkatesh, V., Brown, S.A.: A longitudinal investigation of personal computers in homes: adoption determinants and emerging challenges. MIS Q. **25**(1), 71–102 (2001)

Venkatesh, V., Morris, M.G., Davis, G.B., Davis, F.D.: User acceptance of information technology: toward a unified view. MIS Q. **27**(3), 425–478 (2003)

Wamba, S.F.: Achieving supply chain integration using RFID technology: the case of emerging intelligent B-to-B e-commerce processes in a living laboratory. Bus. Process. Manag. J. **18**(1), 58–81 (2012)

Wang, Y., Kung, L., Byrd, T.A.: Big data analytics: understanding its capabilities and potential benefits for healthcare organizations. Technol. Forecast. Soc. Chang. **126**, 3–13 (2018)

Wang, Y., Kung, L., Gupta, S., Ozdemir, S.: Leveraging big data analytics to improve quality of care in healthcare organizations: a configurational perspective. Br. J. Manag. **30**(2), 362–388 (2019)

Winters, B., et al.: Diagnostic errors in the intensive care unit: a systematic review of autopsy studies. BMJ Qual. Saf. **21**(11), 894–902 (2012)

Wu, I.L., Chen, J.L.: An extension of trust and tam model with TPB in the initial adoption of on-line tax: an empirical study. Int. J. Hum. Comput. Stud. **62**(6), 784–808 (2005)

Yao, W., Chu, C.H., Li, Z.: The adoption and implementation of RFID technologies in healthcare: a literature review. J. Med. Syst. **36**(6), 3507–3525 (2012)

Ye, T.T., et al.: Psychosocial Factors Affecting Artificial Intelligence Adoption in Health Care in China: Cross-Sectional Study. J. Med. Invest. **21**(10), e14316 (2019)

Zhang, F., Li, Z., Zhang, B., Du, H., Wang, B., Zhang, X.: Multi-modal deep learning model for auxiliary diagnosis of Alzheimer's disease. Neurocomputing **361**, 185–195 (2019)

Zhang, C., Ma, R., Sun, S., Li, Y., Wang, Y., Yan, Z.: Optimizing the electronic health records through big data analytics: a knowledge-based view. IEEE Access **7**, 136223–136231 (2019)

Liao, Z., Cheung, M.T.: Internet-based e-shopping and consumer attitudes: an empirical study. Inf. Manag. **38**(5), 299 (2001)

Hierarchical Staffing Problem Under High-Time Varying Demand

Ting Zhang[1], Shuqing Liu[2(✉)], Ping Feng[1], Yali Zheng[1], and Wenge Chen[2]

[1] Guangdong Rail Transit Intelligent Operation and Maintenance Technology Development Center, Shenzhen Technology University, Shenzhen 518118, China
[2] Guangdong University of Technology, Guangzhou 510006, China
liushuqing@mail2.gdut.edu.cn

Abstract. With the increase of the aging population, the nursing homes are becoming more and more important in society. Nursing work has the characteristics of "high time-varying demand, multi shift, hierarchical and collaborative". High time-varying demand means that the demand for personnel varies greatly in each period of 24 h a day; multi shift means that multiple shifts can cover the same time period in a day; hierarchical means that the nurses have different levels; collaborative means different levels of nurses cooperate to serve the elderly. Our work deals with the shift design problem (SDP) and the hierarchical staffing problem, and a two-stage method will be applied. In the first stage, we design shifts according to the high time-varying demand and determine the number of nurses needed for each shift. In the second stage, the constraints of hierarchical collaboration at different levels are considered, and the number of personnel required at different levels for each shift is further determined. Besides, the sensitivity analysis of different demand distribution obtains some meaningful conclusions. Our research results can provide effective decision-making tools and methods for the nursing homes which are facing rapid growth of demand and personnel shortage.

Keywords: Hierarchical staffing · Shift design problem · Nursing homes · Aging population · Healthcare

1 Introduction

With the increasing trend of aging population, the number of the elderly in our country is also increasing fast. The home-based care and nursing homes are the first choice for the elderly, but home-based care has been unable to meet the increasing demand at present. Nursing homes gradually become more and more important in society. However, due to the heavy workload and low wages of the nursing work, many young people are not willing to work in nursing institutions, and it's very hard for the elderly staff to bear such a heavy workload. Simultaneously, the nursing institutions are in a dilemma because of the difficulty in recruiting workers. Besides, most of the nursing homes are manual scheduling, which is not only time-consuming and inefficient, but also leads to the phenomenon of understaffing in peak period and overstaffing in low peak period,

© Springer Nature Singapore Pte Ltd. 2021
Y. Wang et al. (Eds.): DHA 2020, CCIS 1412, pp. 40–51, 2021.
https://doi.org/10.1007/978-981-16-3631-8_5

which causes resource waste. This is a common problem for most nursing homes. What's more, the service quality will be reduced due to the shortage of staff, and the customers will also be reduced, which will decrease the incomes and further lead to the shortage of funds in nursing homes. This will also cause the result of low wages for nurses, which will make it more difficult for nursing homes to recruit workers, and then fall into a vicious circle. Therefore, the nursing homes need an efficient and systematic method to solve the problem of personnel allocation, and make full use of human resources to reduce the waste.

In nursing homes, the work of the professional nurses also have the following characteristics: (1) the number of employees needed within 24 h of a day will change greatly according to different time periods; (2) multiple shifts can be allowed to cover the same time period; (3) employees will be divided into different levels according to their abilities, and an employee with a higher level costs more; (4) different levels of workers can provide different service quality, so we need different levels of workers to cooperate and work together for the elderly. It can be seen from the above characteristics that the arrangement of nursing staff is a complex combination optimization problem. How to deal with the staffing problem efficiently and reasonably under the high time-varying demand has become a difficult problem in nursing institutions. This paper studies these problems existing in nursing homes, and analyzes the impact of high time-varying demand on the shift design results.

The shift design problem (SDP) has been studied by many researches. Musliu [1] divided a day into several periods and Chen [2] studied seasonal demand in commercial banks, and factors such as the demand, understaffing and overstaffing were considered, which is similar to our work. Prot [3] solved the task scheduling problem (TSP) with a two-phase method. In the first phase, shifts were designed according to the time of the task, and tasks were assigned to employees in the second phase. But the time was separated according to tasks, while our problem deals with a consecutive hour in a day. Hierarchical workforce scheduling problem is common in many fields. The TSP Noberto and Volland etc. [4–6] considered the employee's abilities and the employees must have the corresponding abilities to complete the task. But a task only needs one worker instead of collaboration, which is an important factor in our problem. Hadi [7] scheduled a hierarchical workforce with variable demands, and the number of employees who have different levels in each day is predetermined, which is different from our problem as we need to divide a day into several periods. Oezgueven [8] eliminated some shortcomings of the previous model established by Hadi [7], and the new models was evaluated by the case results. However, these models are built without taking into account the fluctuates between different periods of the day. In addition, these problems all assume that a higher qualified worker can substitute for a lower qualified one, but not vice versa. The hierarchical staffing problem in this paper supports that the higher qualified worker can lead the lower qualified worker and needs to meet the constraints of the collaboration of hierarchical employees. Although Alex [9] considered the personnel needed in each time period and the personnel levels, the demand of employees with different levels required in each period is predetermined. While in our problem, the demand of employees with different levels was determined by the constraints of hierarchical collaboration, which is also different from them.

The SDP was solved by set-covering method [10], but it was very difficult to solve because of the large scale of variables. Then, Aykin [11] used an implicit modeling method, which greatly improved the solution results. Since our problem includes shift design and hierarchical collaboration, a two-stage method will be applied. The two-stage method can express the model more easily and distinctly. These papers [2, 12] both described how to use the two-stage method in details, and heuristics and genetic algorithm were suggested to use for these problems [12–14]. In addition, Sana [13] proved the effectiveness of the two-stage method in terms of operation time and solution quality.

To sum up, the problem we described in this paper has the characteristics of high time-varying, multi-shift, hierarchical and collaborative. We will devote to deal with these problems, and the contents will be explained as follows: Sect. 2 gives an overall description and some assumptions of the problem. On this basis, a two-stage model will be described in details in Sect. 3, and genetic algorithm and heuristic are used in the two different stages. Section 4 tests the experimental cases and obtains some meaningful and significant management enlightenment by using sensitivity analysis, and Sect. 5 gives a conclusion about this article and shows some expectations for the future research.

2 Problem Definition

2.1 Overall Description of the Problem

At present, due to the characteristics of nursing work, nursing homes are in a difficult situation of recruitment, which further leads to the lack of funds, and manual scheduling aggravates the problem. Therefore, unreasonable staffing has become the main problem to be solved in nursing homes. Since the work of nurses has the characteristics of high time-varying demand and multi shift, the demand will change greatly according to the different time periods. Manual scheduling is difficult to meet needs, which causes poor service quality due to understaffing and waste of resources because of overstaffing when allocating employees. On the other hand, the nursing work also has the characteristics of hierarchical and collaborative, which means employees will be classified into different levels, and different levels cooperate to serve the elderly. There are many different collocations and nursing homes need to consider reducing cost under the constraints of hierarchical allocation. Manual scheduling is obviously inefficient, so hierarchical collocation is also one of the problems they need to solve. Although the problems are very prominent, an effective solution still has not been found, and this paper will put forward a practical method to solve these problems in nursing homes.

2.2 Assumptions

There are some assumptions for the problem and the details are as follows:

1) The shift can only start and end within the specified time, and the shift can be divided into different types according to the start time, such as morning shift, day shift, afternoon shift and night shift.

2) The duration of each shift should be within 4 h–8 h.
3) One employee can only work one shift a day.
4) Multi shifts are scheduled and allowed to cover the same time period each day.
5) The demand of each period within 24 h of a day may be different, but the needs of each period must be met to avoid the situation of understaffing.
6) Nursing workers have different levels, and the service quality of senior nursing workers is higher than that of junior nursing workers.
7) Junior staff cannot work alone, they must be led by senior staff, and the number of junior staff that a senior staff can lead is limited.
8) Because employees of different levels have different abilities and service quality, so hierarchical collaboration are needed to serve the elderly.
9) The cost of each employee is made up of two parts, one is the shift length, and the other is the employee's level, the employee with a higher level and longer shift length needs more cost.

3 Application of Two-Stage Method

3.1 Global Structure of the Method

Since the nursing homes are facing the problem of unreasonable personnel allocation caused by manual scheduling, which results in the waste of human resources and costs. Therefore, the key to reduce the personnel and cost of nursing homes is to allocate personnel reasonably. First of all, due to the characteristics of high time-varying and multi shift, it is necessary to design shifts reasonably to reduce the waste of human resources. Secondly, we should consider the collocation of personnel at different levels because of the characteristics of hierarchical and collaborative in order to reduce cost as much as possible. On this basis, this paper will adopt a two-stage method. In the first stage, genetic algorithm will be used to design shifts and determine the number of employees needed for each shift according to the high time-varying demand. In the second stage, the shift arrangement determined by the first stage will be considered as a known condition, and the personnel staffing at different levels of each shift will be determined by using rules according to the constraints of hierarchical collaboration.

3.2 Parameter Definition

For the problem in this article, we have the following definitions:

1) t represents the start time of each shift, $t = 0, 1,..., 23$. The shift can only start within the specified time, e.g., if t is 0, the start time of the shift is 0 o 'clock in the evening.
2) h stands for the length of each shift; whose value is between 4 h and 8 h.
3) S represents shift, and S_{th} means a shift which starts at time t and the length is h.
4) K represents the type of shift, when k is 1, 2, 3 and 4, it is classified as morning shift, day shift, afternoon shift and night shift respectively, d_k represents the total number of shift type corresponding to k.

5) Different time periods of one day in 24 h were represented by i, i = 0,1..., 23, e.g., when i is 0, it means that the time period is from 0 p.m. to 1 a.m.
6) b represents the personnel demand, and b_i represents the total personnel demand in each period, where i = 0, 1..., 23. The value of b_i must be an integer.
7) m represents the level of employees, m = 1, 2, 3. When m is 1, 2, 3, it represents senior, intermediate and junior employees respectively.
8) W stands for the number of employees, W_{th} means the total number of nurses in the shift with start time t and length h, and W_{mth} means the total number of nurses in the level m in the shift with start time t and length h.
9) C stands for cost, C_h stands for the cost of a shift with length h, and C_{mh} stands for the cost of an employee whose level is m and shift length is h.
10) n stands for the match ratio of senior and junior employees, e.g., when n is 3, it means that a senior employee can lead at most 3 junior employees.

3.3 Two-Stage Method

3.3.1 First Stage: Shift Design

In first stage, we mainly consider the start time and the length of shifts to reduce the waste of personnel and cost as much as possible while meeting the demand. According to the constraints related to shift arrangement, the number of employees needed in each shift is determined by using genetic algorithm which generates a matrix composed of start time and shift length. The model is established as follows:

$$(IP1) \qquad \min \sum_{t,h} C_h W_{th} S_{th}$$

$$\sum_{t,h} S_{th} W_{th} \geq bi \quad (i = 0, 1, \ldots, 23) \tag{1}$$

$$S_{th} = \begin{cases} 1 \text{ when the shift } S_{th} \text{ includes the time period } i \\ 0 \text{ otherwise} \end{cases}$$

$$\sum_{th \in k} S_{th} \leq d_k (\forall k) \tag{2}$$

$$d_k, W_{th}, b_i \geq 0 \text{ and all integer}$$

In the integer programming model (IP1), the objective function is to minimize the total cost of personnel resources. In this stage, the cost is only related to the shift length, and in these constrains, (1) means that there should have enough employees in each time period to avoid understaffing in peak period. (2) means that the number of different shift types is limited. Different values of k represent different shift types, and the number of shift type corresponding to k cannot exceed d_k.

3.3.2 Second Stage: Hierarchical Collaboration

In second stage, the shift arrangement determined in first stage should be taken as an initial solution, and the constraints of hierarchical collaboration between employees of different levels need to be considered. We should reduce the total cost of staffing as much as possible. Some rules are used in this stage, e.g., the collocation with lower cost have the priority to be adopted. We iterate between the two different stages to improve the quality of the solution, and the model in this stage is as follows:

$$(IP2) \min \sum_{m,t,h} C_{mh} W_{mth}$$

$$\sum_m W_{mth} = S_{th} W_{th} (\forall S_{th} = 1) \tag{3}$$

$$W_{mth} \geq 1 (\forall m; \forall W_{th} \geq 3) \tag{4}$$

$$W_{3th} = 0 (\forall W_{th} = 1) \tag{5}$$

$$W_{3th} \leq n W_{1th} (\forall W_{th} \geq 1) \tag{6}$$

$$W_{mth} \geq 0 \text{ and all integer for } m \in \{1, 2, 3\}$$

Although the objective function also aims to minimize the total cost in this stage, it considers that employees at different levels need different costs. Among these constraints, (3) indicates that the total number of workers at different levels on each shift needs to be equal to the total number of workers on that shift designed in the first stage. (4) means that there should be at least one person in each level when the shift has three or more than three workers. (5) indicates that junior employees cannot be arranged when the shift only has one worker. (6) limits that a senior employee can lead at most n junior employees.

4 Results

4.1 Parameter Setting

We set some parameters for the problems mentioned in this paper:

1. If the cost of an hour is 10, the cost of a shift with four hours (C_4) is 40, and so on.
2. The number of each shift type (morning shift, day shift, afternoon shift and night shift) can't exceed 3. The detailed time schedule of each shift type is shown in Table 1.
3. The cost of one senior, intermediate and junior employee is 100, 70 and 50 respectively, and the total cost of an employee (C_{mh}) is equal to the sum of the employee's level cost and the shift length's cost.
4. One senior worker can lead at most three junior workers, i.e. $n = 3$.
5. The demand of each period(b_i) is irregular, and we will analyze the impact of different demand distributions on the results of shift arrangement.

Table 1. The time arrangement of each shift type

Shift type	Min-start	Max-start	Min-length	Max-length
Morning shift	06:00	08:00	04:00	08:00
Day shift	09:00	11:00	04:00	08:00
Afternoon shift	12:00	16:00	04:00	08:00
Night shift	22:00	00:00	04:00	08:00

4.2 Experiment Results

In the shift scheduling problems, many scholars are committed to reducing the cost or reducing the number of personnel, to some extent, reducing the number of personnel is equivalent to reducing the total personnel cost, which is reflected in many papers [1, 6, 15]. Generally speaking, if the demand is higher, the optimal solution will also need more employees, which will further lead to the increase of the total cost of personnel resources. Although the problem involved in this paper is also aimed at reducing cost, our experimental case needs to meet the characteristics of nursing work in nursing homes.

Since the demand of each period must be an integer, and the high time-varying demand may lead to different demands in different time periods, this paper studies the demand in each period which meets the discrete distribution. In discrete distribution, Poisson distribution and binomial distribution are the most common distributions, and they are often used to solve the problem of meeting customer needs in reality. The key is that they are also applicable to our problems.

According to the high time-varying characteristics of nursing work, we randomly generate a series of discrete demand distributions, which include binomial distribution and Poisson distribution. These generated demand curves meet different means and variances, but all belong to irregular fluctuations. We solve them according to different demand situations, and calculate the total number of employees and total cost in the optimal shift design scheme. Finally, we draw some meaningful conclusions through observing and analyzing the results.

When the demand of each period satisfies the Poisson distribution and binomial distribution, the changes of the total cost are shown in Fig. 1 and Fig. 2 respectively.

According to the pictures above, the following conclusions can be drawn:

1) In Poisson distribution, with the increase of mean value, the total cost shows irregular changes due to the difference of demand distribution in different periods.
2) In binomial distribution, when the variance is constant and the mean value is increasing, the total cost is increasing, but it is nonlinear.
3) In binomial distribution, when the mean value is constant and the variance is gradually increased, the total cost is also gradually increased, but it increased irregularly.

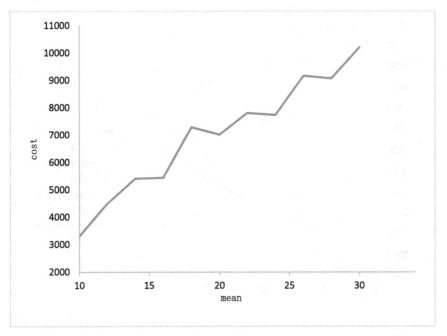

Fig. 1. The changes of the total cost when the demand meets Poisson distribution.

4) In binomial distribution, when the mean value increases gradually, the demand situation with smaller variance needs less cost, and with the increase of mean value, the variance has more significant impact on the total cost.

It can be concluded from the above results that in Poisson distribution, different demand conditions will lead to irregular changes in the total cost, while in binomial distribution, changing the mean and variance will have an obvious and significant impact on the cost.

In addition to the total cost of the optimal shift design scheme, we also make statistics on the personnel arrangement in different distributions, including the minimum and maximum values of the demand in each period. What's more, in order to compare and analyze the personnel arrangement of the optimal shift design scheme more clearly, we also calculate the average value of the personnel demand in each period. The details are shown in Table 2:

Through observing the above table, we can draw the following conclusions:

1) When the demand meets the binomial distribution and the mean value is fixed, the curve with a larger variance has a higher average value of the personnel demand in each period and the total number of employees and the total cost required in the optimal solution are also higher.

2) In Poisson distribution, when the mean value increases gradually, the average value of the personnel demand in each period also shows an ascending trend. However, due to the irregular distribution of demand, the two distributions both appears that

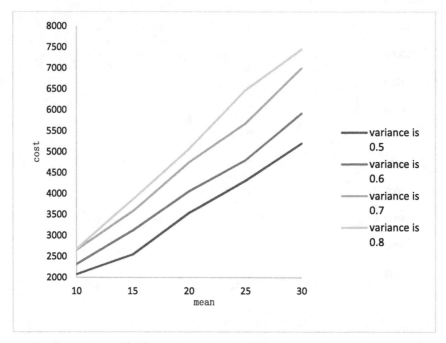

Fig. 2. The changes of the total cost when the demand meets binomial distribution

the higher the average value of the personnel demand in each period, the lower the total number of people and total cost required in the optimal solution.

3) In Poisson distribution, due to the irregularity of demand distribution and the difference of employee's level, it can be found that the higher the total number of employees needed in the optimal solution, the lower the total cost.

4.3 Discussions and Summaries

According to the above experimental test results, when the nursing work has the characteristics of high time-varying demand, the total number of employees and the total cost required will arise with the increase of the average value of the personnel demand in each period, but it's not linear growth. In addition, because of the irregularity of demand distribution, it may happen that a higher demand may need less employees. This is opposite of the result that a higher demand needs more employees in shift design. Besides, the cases above also show that more employees may need less cost, which is also opposite of the most shift design results that more employees need a higher cost. To sum up, due to the characteristics of nursing work in nursing homes, the total number of employees and the total cost needed in the optimal shift design scheme will change with the high time-varying demand, and different demand distributions have different degrees of influence on the optimal solution, and the conclusions obtained from the experiments are also significant and meaningful.

Table 2. Personnel arrangement under different distributions

Distribution	Mean	Variance	The minimum demand	The maximum demand	The average demand	The optimal solution	
						Number	Cost
Binomial distribution	10	0.5	2	9	5.44	16	2080
		0.6	2	9	6.37	17	2320
		0.7	5	10	7.81	19	2660
		0.8	6	10	8.56	19	2680
	15	0.5	3	10	6.81	19	2550
		0.6	6	11	8.87	22	3120
		0.7	7	13	10.75	26	3580
		0.8	9	14	11.94	28	3860
	20	0.5	4	15	8.81	27	3540
		0.6	9	15	11.75	30	4060
		0.7	11	18	14.5	34	4750
		0.8	13	18	16	36	5070
	25	0.5	9	16	12.56	31	4310
		0.6	11	17	14.69	34	4800
		0.7	15	21	18.44	40	5680
		0.8	15	24	19.56	47	6470
	30	0.5	9	19	14.87	38	5200
		0.6	11	22	17.62	43	5920
		0.7	17	27	21.31	52	7000
		0.8	22	28	24.12	53	7450
Poisson distribution	10		5	16	9.88	24	3310
	12		5	17	11.37	34	4500
	14		9	21	14.31	41	5410
	16		11	22	16	40	5450
	18		10	27	19.31	53	7290
	20		14	26	20.44	51	7020
	22		11	34	19.94	59	7810
	24		16	31	23.19	56	7740

(continued)

Table 2. (*continued*)

Distribution	Mean	Variance	The minimum demand	The maximum demand	The average demand	The optimal solution	
						Number	Cost
	26	19	33	25.44	66	9160
	28	23	34	29.44	64	9070
	30	14	37	30.56	74	10210

5 Conclusions

This paper mainly describes the difficulties faced by nursing homes at present, and applies a two-stage method to solve the problem according to the nurses' work characteristics of multi shift, high time-varying, hierarchical and collaborative. Genetic algorithm is used at the first stage for shift design and the rules are applied at the second stage for hierarchical collaborative respectively. Finally, this paper also gives the sensitivity analysis of different demand distributions, and the demands of different time periods which meet the Poisson distribution and binomial distribution are tested. The results show that the irregular demand fluctuation has an obvious effect on the optimal shift design scheme. Because of the working characteristics of nurses, the optimal solution is quite different from the most shift design results. This paper puts forward a feasible method to solve the problem in nursing homes and tests many different cases, and the conclusions are also meaningful, which has a certain enlightenment and rich significance to solve the real problems.

Acknowledgments. This work is supported by National Natural Science Foundation of China (71701052), Guangdong Natural Science Foundation (2017C030110189), Shenzhen High-Caliber Personnel Research Start-up Project (2020111), Ordinary University Engineering Technology Development Center Project of Guangdong Province(2019GCZX006), Shenzhen Technology University Teaching Reform Project, Guangzhou Yuexiu science and technology plan project (2017-GX-005).

References

1. Musliu, N., Schaerf, A., Slany, W.: Local search for shift design. Eur. J. Oper. Res. **153**(1), 51–64 (2004)
2. Chen, Y., Zhang, X., Bian, B., Li, H.: Optimal staffing policy in commercial banks under seasonal demand variation. IEEE Access **7**, 121111–121126 (2019)
3. Prot, D., Lapègue, T., Bellenguez-Morineau, O.: A two-phase method for the shift design and personnel task scheduling problem with equity objective. Int. J. Prod. Res. **53**(24), 1–13 (2015)
4. Hernández-Leandro, N.A., Boyer, V., Salazar-Aguilar, M.A.: A matheuristic based on Lagrangian relaxation for the multi-activity shift scheduling problem. Eur. J. Oper. Res. 859–867 (2019)

5. Volland, J., Fügener, A., Brunner, J.O.: A column generation approach for the integrated shift and task scheduling problem of logistics assistants in hospitals. Eur. J. Oper. Res. **260**(1), 316–334 (2017)
6. Hojati, M.: A greedy heuristic for shift minimization personnel task scheduling problem. Comput. Oper. Res. 66–76 (2018)
7. Seckiner, S.U., Hadi, G., Kurt, M.: An integer programming model for hierarchical workforce scheduling problem. Eur. J. Oper. Res. **183**(2), 694–699 (2007)
8. Oezgueven, C., Sungur, B.: Integer programming models for hierarchical workforce scheduling problems including excess off-days and idle labour times. Appl. Math. Model. 9117–9131 (2013)
9. Bonutti, A., Ceschia, S., De, F., et al.: Modeling and solving a real-life multi-skill shift design problem. Ann. Oper. Res. **252**, 365–382 (2017)
10. Dantzig, G.B.: A comment on Edie's "traffic delays at toll booths" (letter). J. Oper. Res. Soc. Am. **2**(3), 339–341 (1954)
11. Aykin, T.: Optimal shift scheduling with multiple break windows. Manag. Sci. **42**(4), 591–602 (1996)
12. Lequy, Q., Desaulniers, G., Solomon, M.M.: A two-stage heuristic for multi-activity and task assignment to work shifts. Comput. Ind. Eng. **63**(4), 831–841 (2012)
13. Dahmen, S., Rekik, M., Soumis, F.: A two-stage solution approach for personalized multi-department multi-day shift scheduling. Eur. J. Oper. Res. 1051–1063 (2020)
14. Pakpoom, P., Charnsethikul, P.: A column generation approach for personnel scheduling with discrete uncertain requirements. In: 2nd International Conference on Informatics and Computational Sciences (ICICoS), Semarang, Indonesia, pp. 1–6 (2018)
15. Di Gaspero, L., Gaertner, J., Kortsarz, G., Musliu, N.: The minimum shift design problem. Ann. Oper. Res. **155**(1), 79–105 (2007)

Research on the Demands of the Elderly in the Community Home-Based Care Model

Aobo Lyu[1], Xian Cheng[2], Ying Zhao[1(✉)], Liang Zhou[1], and Hongjiao Fu[3]

[1] School of Public Administration, Sichuan University, Chengdu, China
Zhaoying@scu.edu.cn
[2] Business School, Sichuan University, Chengdu, China
[3] School of Information, Renmin University of China, Beijing, China

Abstract. The community home-based care service, which refers to integrating the service resources around the community to provide elderly care service in the community, has become one of the dominant elderly service models. The effective integration of various resources around the community at the infancy stage of community home-based care service has a significant impact on the operation costs of elderly services institutions. However, the suitability of resource integration is highly dependent on the service demands for the elderly in community. Thus, obtaining accurate service demands for the elderly is very important in the development of the community home-based care service. In this paper, we focus on exploring the service demands of the elderly. First, we conduct a structured questionnaire survey of 2200 elderly in Fangshan District, Beijing, and collect the elderly's demographic information and their community home-based care service demands. Second, we establish a service demand model, which presents the relationship between demographic information and the demands of community home-based care service, by using a business intelligence technique—decision tree to analyze the data. The result shows different demographic characteristics jointly affect the elderly's community home-based care service demands and concludes the demand feature of three particular types of community home-based care services: door to door service, community medical service, and community non-medical service. This study illustrates that through the analysis of the elderly's demographic data, we can effectively obtain the service demands for the elderly, and thus can more effectively integrate resources and improve the development efficiency of the community home-based care industry. This study also expands the research on elderly service by establishing a service demand model.

Keywords: Community home-based care · Elderly service · Data analysis · Decision tree

1 Introduction

The trend of population aging is increasingly becoming a major challenge for many advanced economies in the world. China has also entered the ranks of these aging countries according to the standard set by the World Health Organization. The rapid growth

© Springer Nature Singapore Pte Ltd. 2021
Y. Wang et al. (Eds.): DHA 2020, CCIS 1412, pp. 52–65, 2021.
https://doi.org/10.1007/978-981-16-3631-8_6

of the aging population has made the provision of sufficient long-term care (LTC) services for older people a critical social problem. In order to forecast the demand for LTC services and related costs, it is necessary to explore and make theoretical sense of older people's LTC needs and to identify the factors that influence them (Mueller 2000).

At present, the mainstream LTC model in the world is institutional care. For traditional institutional care, developed countries have already built up relatively advanced service delivery systems for older people's institutional care, and there are also comprehensive government policies and regulations to monitor the quality of service delivery, for example, the White Paper "Caring for Our Future: Reforming Care and Support" in England, the Act on Prevention of Elderly Abuse and Support for Attendants of Elderly Persons in Japan, the Omnibus Budget Reconciliation Act of 1987 in the US. In China, institutional care is still in short supply compared with that in the developed countries. Nursing homes can provide beds for only 2.72% of the total number of older people. (Ministry of Civil Affair of the People's Republic of China 2015). Based on the current situation, Community home-based care service has gradually become the first choice for the elderly in China (Li and Wan 2020).

The community home-based care model is a socialized elderly service model (Mosquera 2018) involves home-based, community-based, door to door service and community daycare, and introduces professional services by elderly service institutions. Nowadays, community home-based care services have become a dominant international elderly service model (Huang 2013). Although the lack of adequate and affordable institutional care and the weakening of traditional family care have made community home-based care an appealing option, in China, community home-based care is still at the early stages compared with that in developed countries. China is facing challenges regarding how to address mounting service needs with limited social resources in a young, developing civil society (Xu and Chow 2011). For instance, it still faces many challenges in the integration of service resources around the community, the operation of home-based care service, and the construction of software and hardware environment (Bai and Niu 2013). Among them, the core problem faced by the community home-based care service industry in the early implementation stage is the efficiency of service resource integration. Community home-based care service demands to go beyond the community's space and integrate the resources of care service around the community. However, the suitability of resource integration is highly dependent on the service demands for the elderly in community. Thus, obtaining accurate service demands for the elderly is very important in the development of the community home-based care service.

However, nowadays, elderly services institutions can only use user feedback to obtain elderly service demands after providing elderly services to users (Cappanera et al. 2018), making it hard to integrate the resource around the community effectively. This situation leads to the fact that elderly services institutions have to constantly adjust the resource integration tactics based on the user's feedback, which makes elderly services institutions pay a higher cost in the early stage. Moreover, because the elderly in different communities have significant differences in their home-based care service demands (Yan and Gao 2013), it is impossible to apply the resource integration tactics of one community to the other community. Therefore, how to accurately obtain the service demands of the elderly is a key issue in the development of community home-based care service mode, which is also the problem that this study wants to explore. In order to effectively integrate resources and reduce operation costs, elderly services institutions need to use different approaches to obtain the service demands of the elderly accurately and in time. Nowadays, more and more cities begin to build smart cities and collect basic information and establish archives for the elderly (Hepburn 2018), these data which contains much useful information, e.g., demographic information, which provides a new solution for elderly services institutions to obtain service demands for the elderly. Elderly services institutions can use demographic information to analyze the demands of the elderly in a community before providing elderly services in the community. However, the prerequisite for this solution is the feasibility of establishing a service demand model, which presents the relationship between demographic information and the demands of community home-based care service.

Previous studies have shown that there is an apparent relationship between the demographic characteristics and demand for elderly services (Chu et al. 2007). As the demands of the elderly are generally related, we have reason to believe that there is a certain relationship between the demands of the elderly in the community home-based care model and their demographic information. Therefore, the first task of the study is to verify that community home-based care service demands of the elderly can be obtained through the analysis of the elderly demographic information. In addition, based on verifying the feasibility of this solution, the study also obtains the general conclusion about the elderly community home-based elderly care service demand through this analysis method. Specifically, we focus on: What kind of demographic data should be used to analyze the demands of different types of community home-based elderly care services? What is the priority of different demographic data? What is the special relationship between different demographic data and demands? And how should enterprises and governments make use of these connections to formulate community home-based pension development strategies better and provide better services?

The remainder of this paper is structured as follows: In Sect. 1, we reviewed relevant research in the field of home-based care and identified the types of services and demographic characteristics that affect the demands of the elderly. In Sect. 2, we provide details about the data used for this research project, as well as the empirical approach employed. In Sect. 3, we highlight the findings of this study, while those are discussed in Sect. 4. Additionally, contributions to both theory and practice, as well as limitations, are pointed out. A conclusion wraps up the key takeaways of this paper.

2 Literature Review

The research on home-based elderly care mainly focuses on the research of home-based care mode for the elderly. Recently, some studies began to use data analysis methods to analyze the life of the elderly in community home-based care modle. We can notice that many compelling studies are using AI, machine learning or data analysis methods to analyze the elderly in the home-based care model (Yuan et al. 2020; Veyron et al. 2019; Jacobs 2018). However, the demand analysis of the elderly in the community home mode is still in a blank state. To better understand the analysis of the demands of the elderly under the community home-based care model for the aged based on demographic information, this section will review and sort out the previous studies from the current services of community home-based care model and the influence factors of elderly's demands, and obtain the dependent variables and independent variable candidates required for this study.

2.1 Current Services of Community Home-Based Care Model

Community home-based care for the elderly is a model of integrating community and surrounding resources to provide services for the elderly. There are many types of community home-based care services. Therefore, it is necessary to clearly define the service scope of community-based elderly care mode and accurately divide the service types for in-depth demand analysis. By reviewing the existing research in related fields, we can have a framework judgment and classification of the community home care service model.

From the perspective of service personnel, some studies have pointed out that there are two main occupations associated with the direct care of people in their homes: personal care aides also called home care aides or personal care assistants, and home health aides. There is a significant overlap in the roles of these two types of aides (Spetz et al. 2019). The majority of the care services involve support with personal care—including bathing, dressing, grooming, using the toilet, eating, moving around, cleaning the house, preparing food, and taking medications (Hardy 2014).

Community non-medical service is a kind of on-site service provided by the community service center; research found that the critical factor affecting the satisfaction of the elderly is the service quality of the service center (Li and Wan 2020). Therefore, the community non-medical service should be regarded as the second type of service, different from door-to-door service.

Based on the existing literature, we can divide the community home-based care into the following three types according to the factors of service personnel, service location and served role: door-to-door service, community non-medical service, and community medical service.

2.2 Influence Factors of Elderly's Demands

More and more people begin to pay attention to the demographic information about the factors that affect the demands of the elderly and have obtained ideal results. Previous studies have roughly shown that the main factors affecting the demands of elderly services are age, marital status, education level, occupation, medical security form, family economic status, number of pensions, self-care ability, living in urban or rural areas (Chu et al. 2007). Some scholars also said that the elderly should be classified according to age, physical condition, income level, education level, and other factors within the community home-based care mode to meet the demands of different levels of the elderly (Zhang and Zhao 2011). Among them, basic characteristics such as age and gender have been verified to be more sensitive in influencing the demands of the elderly for long-term care (Fu et al. 2017). A highly effective study on changes in community-based care use determined by health, personal, and facilitating factors was conducted in the Netherlands from 2004 to 2011. The research has shown that the influence of income and household composition on demand for elderly community home-based care has changed the most, and to a lesser extent, the role of age and physical impairments. Care use decreased among individuals with high incomes and increased among single persons (The changes in community-based care use and in the role of income and household composition could be due to changes in eligibility for care.) (Plaisier et al. 2017). In terms of medical needs, some studies have pointed out that some demographic information will reflect the disease situation of the elderly, such as client lives with primary caregiver; Older age (65 years and older); marital status; the client now lives with other persons, etc., (Pauley et al. 2018) and these factors will indirectly affect the community medical needs of the elderly (Zhao et al. 2017). Similarly, demographic data such as social support, functional status (self-care ability), and health care use are also involved in predicting the home health status of the elderly (Hsu et al. 2016).

3 Materials and Methods

In this section, we provide an elaboration of the (suitability of the) data we use to analyze the research topics. Furthermore, we describe the variables included in our model. Subsequently, we highlight the empirical approach employed in this paper.

3.1 Data and Sample

To explore the relationship between basic information and demand information of the elderly, we make use of the Beijing Fangshan District Elderly service Survey. The Survey is a harmonized survey of home-based care circumstances of the elderly, collected biannually in member street of Fangshan District, Beijing, China, collected jointly by the Beijing Lelaohui Elderly Service Co., Ltd. For this study, we make use of the Survey of elderly in 31 communities in four streets of Fangshan District with 2210 questionnaires.

The reasons why the Survey an appropriate source of data for the research at hand are twofold. On the one hand, the Survey as a secondary source of data has several advantages over primary data, for instance, providing information about the elderly can avoid the elderly's resistance to collecting information in the name of the individual. On the other hand, based on ensuring the reliability of the data, obtaining relevant information from the census can also avoid the subjective tendency or suggestiveness of the experiment in the questionnaire design.

3.2 Variables

Dependent Variables. Based on the division of community home-based care model service types in the first section of the study, we collected the demand degree of the elderly for these three types of services: Door-to-door service, community non-medical service and community medical service. By asking the elderly some questions about community home-based care services, we obtained the elderly's demand for different services. Accurately, the degree of the community medical service, community non-medical service, and door to door services required by the elderly is characterized by the average score (1–5 demand-level) of the 5, 9, and 11 certain services, respectively. The details are as follows:

Community medical service is a basic elderly service provided by a community hospital or clinic. Five services represent it in the questionnaire. They are 'physician's regular health consultation,' 'regularly accompany the doctor, and receive prescription drugs,' 'Regular door to door rehabilitation training service,' 'Regular health check-up and ability assessment,' and 'Infusion and blood pressure measurement.'

Community non-medical service is a type of service based on a specific scenario of a community that is taken care of by a community agency or a nonprofit organization. Nine services represent it in the questionnaire. They are 'senior care station and senior daycare service,' 'senior care station of psychological counseling and comfort service,' 'senior care station of old man bathhouse,' 'elderly chess and card room,' 'organize entertainment or outing activities,' 'organize interest classes,' 'training classes,' 'travel planning and transportation assistance,' 'legal consultation and matchmaking service.'

Door to door service is a kind of service from the community's periphery, integrated by the community elderly service platform. Eleven services represent it in the questionnaire. They are 'Bath and body scrubbing,' 'personal cleaning (haircut and pedicure),' 'purchasing daily necessities and food,' 'household cleaning,' 'sanitation and disinfection,' 'washing and finishing of large items or clothing,' 'customization of independent living aids,' 'renovation of home accessibility facilities,' 'food delivery services,' 'housekeeping maintenance services,' 'elderly health massage and pedicure,' and '24-hour emergency assistance'.

The final score of community medical service, community non-medical service, and door to door service is the average of those service demands. The specific correspondence is shown in Table 1.

Table 1. Dependent variable value

Dependent variables	0	1	2	3	4	5
Degree of demand for door to door service	No need	Optional	Recognized	Demand	Strong demand	Necessary
Degree of demand for community medical service	No need	Optional	Recognized	Demand	Strong demand	Necessary
Degree of demand for community non-medical service	No need	Optional	Recognized	Demand	Strong demand	Necessary

Independent Variables. Based on the conclusions of the first section of the study, in order to explore the relationship between different demographic data and the needs of the elderly more comprehensively, we selected 12 representative demographic information of the elderly as the analysis object, which are gender, age, location of household registration, education level, self-care ability, spouse status, living conditions, number of children, number of parents, income, and source of income, and number of house properties.

Among them, the surveyed elderly are all 60 years old and above. The household registration only asks whether it is Beijing household registration. The level of education is represented by the highest level of education received. The self-care evaluation criteria are based on whether the elderly need help from others in their daily lives. Self-care ability is divided into three levels: self-care, semi-self-care, and unable to self-care. The spouse situation is based on the latest spouse situation. The number of children is based on the number of children in the legal name, and the number of parents is included in the statistics of living parents and spouse parents. The income is subject to RMB income after tax. The source of income only distinguishes whether it is income from personal work, investment, or whether it is a gift from others, such as children or relatives.

Among them, gender and location of household registration are measured as a binary variable, and the remaining features are measured as integers ranging from 1–3 to 1–9. The specific correspondence is shown in Table 2.

Control Variables. The elderly's conditions and living conditions collected in this experiment are not the only factors determining the elderly's choices about elderly services; we include a list of control variables in our study. As highlighted by Some methodological aspects of using postal questionnaires with the elderly, the elderly's active completion rate for long questionnaires is significantly affected by their age (Victor 1988). Therefore, we control the way of data acquisition, and all the methods of questionnaire acquisition are in the form of interviews conducted by investigators.

Additionally, we also include a control measure for the same growth environment. Due to the fundamental values and worldview of a group affect the nature of its members' beliefs and practices around health and illness (Barker 1995). This study tries to avoid the impact of different cultural backgrounds on the elderly, which is difficult to measure quantitatively. The data used in this study comes from a specific street in Fangshan District, Beijing, a place with little population migration due to historical reasons.

3.3 Empirical Approach

In this study, we use the ID3 decision tree algorithm to establish the relationship model between the elderly demographic data and the elderly community home-based care demands. Decision Tree is an important method for both induction research and data mining, which is mainly used for model classification and prediction. ID3 algorithm is the most widely used algorithm in the decision tree so far (Jin et al. 2009). In recent years, there are also researches on the analysis of the elderly using Decision Tree for characteristics analysis (Park 2018). By establishing a decision tree, we can categorize different kinds of users, and sort the different independent variables according to their influence priority (Safavian and Landgrebe 1991). In this study, twelve demographic data are used as independent variables for the input of the decision tree model training, and three community home-based care service demands are used as dependent variables for the prediction results of the model. By limiting the number of layers and cutting off

Table 2. Independent variable value

Independent variables	Number	0	1	2	3	4	5	6	7
Gender	X [0]	Female	Male	-	-	-	-	-	-
Age	X [1]	60–69	70–79	80–89	90+	-	-	-	-
Household registration	X [2]	Beijing	Others	-	-	-	-	-	-
Education level	X [3]	Elementary school and below	Junior high school	Technical secondary school or high school	College, university and above	-	-	-	-
Self-care ability	X [4]	Self-care	Semi-self-care	Unable to self-care	-	-	-	-	-
Spouse status	X [5]	With spouse	Widowed	Divorced	Unmarried	-	-	-	-
People living together	X [6]	Alone	Relatives only	Children only	Spouse only	Children and spouse	-	-	-
Number of children	X [7]	0	1	2	3	4	5	6	7+
Number of parents	X [8]	0	1	2	3	4+	-	-	-
Income	X [9]	0–999	1k–1999	2k–2999	3k–3999	4k–4999	5k–5999	6k+	-
Source of income	X [10]	Personal income	Others give	-	-	-	-	-	-
Personal housing	X [11]	Have	Don't have	-	-	-	-	-	-

the branches with a small sample size in the process of establishing the decision tree, we finally get three classification trees of community home-based care service demand based on the elderly demographic data. The data analysis tools of this study are Excel and Python. By cleaning the original questionnaire results, we obtained the independent variables and dependent variables required by this research. Then, the data analysis algorithm is implemented through python programming to analyze the data.

4 Results

The data analysis results of this study can be divided into three topics according to the dependent variables selected in the study, namely community medical service demand, community non-medical service demand, and door to door service demand. Figures 1, 2, and 3 present the results of our analyses.

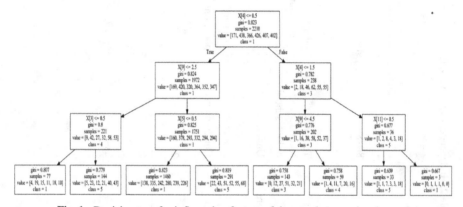

Fig. 1. Decision tree for influencing factors of door to door service demand

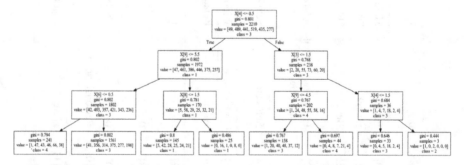

Fig. 2. Decision tree for influencing factors of community non-medical service demand

Figure 1 presents the analysis of door to door service demand. Through the Fig. 1, we can find that the ability of the elderly to take care of themselves (X [4]) is the decisive factor that affects the elderly's demand for door to door service. The elderly with self-care ability has no demand for door to door service. The demand for door to door service

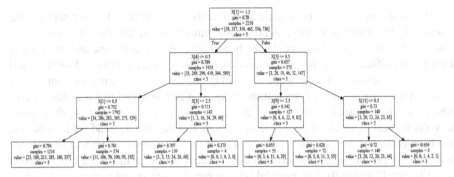

Fig. 3. Decision tree for influencing factors of community medical service demand

of semi-self-care and unable-self-care elderly is increasing in turn. It is worth noting that, like common sense, older people with lower incomes (X [9]) are not willing to purchase services, but older people with lower incomes and higher education (X [3]) have more demand for door to door service. Conversely, even if the income is relatively higher if the spouse is healthy (X [5]), then the elderly would prefer to manage their own lives instead of buying door to door services.

Figure 2 presents the analysis of community non-medical service demand. Like the home service model, the elderly's demand for community non-medical service is mainly affected by the elderly's self-care level (X [4]). It is worth noting that although elderly with higher self-care levels are generally not interested in community non-medical service, those with lower incomes (X [9]) and relatively lonely (X [6]) people have a higher demand for community non-medical service.

Figure 3 presents the analysis of community medical service demand. As is generally believed, the older the elderly (X [1]), the higher the demand for community medical service, which is particularly evident in the community medical service demand table. Also, the education level (X [3]) and self-care ability (X [4]) have a more significant impact. However, As the elderly collected in the questionnaire generally have a strong demand for community medical service, the analysis did not reflect a significant difference.

5 Discussion

Through this model, we can roughly find that there are high correlations between the elderly's general demands and some individual characteristics, such as income, age, self-care ability, partner status, and education level. Moreover, other characteristics, such as the number of children, the number of parents, the location of the household registration, and whether or not they have house also affect the demands of the elderly to a certain extent. Besides, we realize that any basic characteristics of the elderly are not monotonously positively or negatively related to a certain demand of the elderly. The change of some basic characteristics will produce different demand results under different conditions. Therefore, only by collecting enough basic information of the elderly can the demand analysis result be more accurate. On this basis, this study also summarizes the influencing factors of three different community-home-based care services.

By comparing the results of the demand analysis of the door to door service, the community non-medical service, and the community medical service can be found that although the three types of services have a high degree of overlap in time and space, there are apparent differences in the audiences of the three services. The door to door service is equivalent to the elderly's daily work, and will gradually become the mainstream service model. According to the analysis results in Fig. 1, it can be found that the older people who do not have sufficient labor force in the family and can not meet the daily work have the highest demand for door to door service. Besides, the demand for low-income and high-education people also proves that door to door service is not just choices for high-income people, which means that door to door service will have a broad market in the future. Community non-medical service mainly correspond to the social contact demands of the elderly, and this kind of community non-medical service is regarded as a low-level substitute for daily social interaction. According to the analysis results in Fig. 2, it can be found that the elderly who are lack social activities in daily life is more willing to participate in community activities. Simultaneously, because low-income people pay more attention to community non-medical service, service providers should appropriately reduce the cost and price of such services to cater to the major consumer groups in the market. The community medical service solves the problem of a broad range of non-targeted medical demands. From the analysis results in Fig. 3, it can be found that the demand for community medical service for the elderly is generally high and is highly related to age, which means that the community medical service should meet the non-targeted basic medical demands.

Implication for the Theory. First of all, this study verifies the previous research conclusions in the community home-based care model; that is, the elderly's demands can be obtained by analyzing the elderly's demographic information of the elderly. On this basis, it is found that the relationship between a single demographic data of the elderly and a certain demand is not monotonous. Under the condition of different other demographic characteristics, the change of a demographic characteristic is not consistent with the change in the elderly's demands. Only by comprehensive analysis of a variety of basic information of the elderly, can we better grasp the specific demands of the elderly. Besides, this study also established the relationship model of key demographic variables and demands for three groups of demand variables. The model can well show the influence degree of different demographic variables and the specific demands of the elderly under different conditions made up of other demographic characteristics.

Implication for the Practice. Besides contribution to theory, our research also has implications for practitioners. As mentioned earlier, the three types of home-based care services have different market positioning and target groups. Enterprises should adopt differentiated market strategies for different service types. Specifically, the door to door service type should be developed towards a shared and personalized service model. While reducing the price, the service content should cover the daily life of the elderly as much as possible. The development of community non-medical service should focus on the low-cost realization of social needs. By providing a platform to attract the elderly in the community to socialize, it should focus on the essence of social services while ensuring low prices. In the area of community medical service, large-scale non-targeted medical service capabilities should be guaranteed, take the construction of community medical service as the main driving force of the popularization of the community home-based care model.

In a nutshell, we show that it is essential for firms to be aware of the differences in elderly's demands for elderly care services in different regions, and collect basic information about elderly in this community from government departments or certain organization before entering a community, and determine the general demands of elderly in the community. Integrate cost-effective service resources as much as possible to reduce the cost of starting the industry. Besides, government departments should provide specific help to enterprises in terms of information, such as building an information platform for the elderly, partially opening anonymous data for the elderly, and assisting companies to conduct elderly data surveys.

Limitation and Future Research. Despite providing some insights about demand analysis for the elderly at the community home-based care model, this study also duffers from a few limitations. Those are mainly related to the fact that research based on the current questionnaire results. Namely, it is a survey-based data collection method, entailing potential biases such as self-selection. As the questionnaire survey is conducted in a specific area, it suffers from history and population migration; we might not be able to work with an entirely random sample. Furthermore, the questions in the Beijing Fangshan District Elderly service Survey are not specialized in this study but fit a rather wide variety of research projects. This means that we often face restrictions on terms of variable measurement and consistency, for instance. Due to such a restriction, the study at hand can only represent the selection mode of the elderly in local areas. If we want the conclusion to be widely adopted in a broader range, it is necessary to obtain more extensive data for analysis.

Nevertheless, these issues could be addressed by future research. Using additional data sources, e.g., interviews or case studies could shed more light on the results produces in this study. Mainly, with the advancement of the National Social Science Fund project that supports this research, we will get more extensive and targeted information in the future.

6 Conclusions

This paper studies the relationship between the demographic information of the elderly and their demands of community home-based care services. Combined with the conclusions of previous studies, this study proves that the elderly's community home-based care demands can be obtained by analyzing the demographic information of the elderly. Based on the previous research on the correlation between a single independent variable and dependent variable in the field of elderly service (Huang 2015), this study proposes that there is a complicated conditional relationship between the elderly demography and their demands, only a combination of multiple demographic variables can jointly reflect the elderly's demand for certain elderly services. Only by comprehensive analysis of a variety of demographic data, can we get accurate elderly care demand. In addition to verifying the feasibility of the data analysis process, this study also constructs a relationship model between the demographics data and the demands of community home-based care services. Through the model, enterprises can accurately determine the elderly's community home-based care service demands according to the collected demographic data of the elderly, to more accurately integrate resources.

With this research, we contribute to theory as we shed more light on and advance the general understanding of the concept of the relationship between the basic characteristics of the elderly and the demands of the elderly in the community. At the same time, the research also has practical significance. This study proposes a model of elderly demand in the home-based elderly care industry through data analysis methods that apply business intelligence and makes contributions to the current elderly demands analysis conclusions. Besides, the paper affirms the importance of the construction of an information platform for the elderly in the construction of digital government from the perspective of the government. Moreover, from the perspective of the enterprise, the study provides an analysis model for the analysis of the demands of start-up companies and transformation companies in the home-based care industry and then provide guidance and help in resource allocation to provide future personalized elderly service models for community home-based care ideas and insights.

Nowadays, the issue of the aging population is getting more and more attention. The analysis of the demands of the elderly under the community home-based care model can guide enterprises in the market analysis and become a support for the development of government elderly service work. We hope to contribute to the elderly care career through this research.

References

Barker, J.C.: Recognizing cultural differences: Health-care providers and elderly patients. Gerontol. Geriatr. Educ. **15**(1), 9–22 (1995)

Yan, B., Gao, X.: Influencing factors of urban elderly people's home-satisfaction satisfaction and community differences. Geograph. Res. **32**(07), 1269–1279 (2013)

Jin, C., De-Lin, L., Fen-Xiang, M.: An improved ID3 decision tree algorithm. In: 2009 4th International Conference on Computer Science & Education, pp. 127–130. IEEE (2009)

Victor, C.R.: Some methodological aspects of using postal questionnaires with the elderly. Arch. Gerontol. Geriatr. **7**(2), 163–172 (1988)

Mosquera, F., Smet, P., Berghe, G.V.: Flexible home-based care scheduling. Omega **83**, 80–95 (2018)

Huang, F.-H.: Explore home-based care needs and satisfaction for elderly people with chronic disease and their family members. Procedia Manuf. **3**, 173–179 (2015)

Fu, Y.Y., Guo, Y., Bai, X., Chui, E.W.T.: Factors associated with older people's long-term care needs: a case study adopting the expanded version of the Anderson model in China. BMC Geriatr. **17**(1), 38 (2017)

Hardy, S.E.: Consideration of function and functional decline. In: Williams, B.A., Chang, A., Ahalt, C., Chen, H., Conant, R., Landefeld, C.S., et al. (eds.) Current Diagnosis and Treatment: Geriatrics, 2nd edn, pp. 3–4. McGraw-Hill, New York (2014)

Hepburn, P.A.: A new governance model for delivering digital policy agendas: a case study of digital inclusion amongst elderly people in the UK. Int. J. E-Plan. Res. (IJEPR) **7**(3), 36–49 (2018)

Hsu, A.T., et al.: Algorithm for predicting death among older adults in the home care setting: study protocol for the risk evaluation for support: predictions for elder-life in the community tool (RESPECT). BMJ Open 6(12), (2016)

Jacobs, S.: Genetic algorithm for schedule optimization in the homecare industry (2018)

Li, T., Wan, L.: A study of influencing factors of satisfaction of community home-based nursing service based on ACSI model. In: 2020 International Conference on Advanced Education, Management and Information Technology, AEMIT 2020, pp. 57–60. Atlantis Press (2020)

Ministry of Civil Affair of the People's Republic of China. Statistics on the Development of Social Services in 2014 (2015). Accessed 29 Mar 2016. http://www.mca.gov.cn/article/zwgk/mzyw/201506/20150600832371.shtml

Mueller, C.: The RUG-III case mix classification system for long-term care nursing facilities: is it adequate for nurse staffing? J. Nurs. Adm. 30, 535–543 (2000)

Cappanera, P., Scutellà, M.G., Nervi, F., Galli, L.: Demand uncertainty in robust home-based care optimization. Omega 80, 95–110 (2018)

Park, M.-Y.: Determinant of the elderly poverty using decision tree analysis. J. Digit. Converg. 16(7), 63–69 (2018)

Pauley, T., Chang, B.W., Wojtak, A., Seddon, G., Hirdes, J.: Predictors of caregiver distress in the community setting using the home care version of the resident assessment instrument. Prof. Case Manag. 23(2), 60–69 (2018)

Bai, P., Niu, G.: Development ideas and countermeasures of home-based elderly care services in urban communities. City Watch (04), 33–44 (2013). https://doi.org/0.3969/j.issn.674-778.203.04.004

Plaisier, I., Verbeek-Oudijk, D., de Klerk, M.: Developments in home-care use. Policy and changing community-based care use by independent community-dwelling adults in the Netherlands. Health Policy 121(1), 82–89 (2017)

Zhang, Q., Zhao, Q.: Study on the model of home-based community caring for the elderly. J. Northeast. Univ. (Soc. Sci.) 5, 416–420+425 (2011)

Huang, S.: Characteristics of home-based care services for foreign urban communities. Urban Probl. (08), 83–88 (2013). https://doi.org/10.13239/j.bjsshkxy.cswt.2013.08.018

Spetz, J., Stone, R.I., Chapman, S.A., Bryant, N.: Home and community-based workforce for patients with serious illness requires support to meet growing needs. Health Aff. 38(6), 902–909 (2019)

Safavian, S.R., Landgrebe, D.: A survey of decision tree classifier methodology. IEEE Trans. Syst. Man Cybern. 21(3), 660–674 (1991). https://doi.org/10.1109/21.97458

Veyron, J.H., et al.: Home care aides' observations and machine learning algorithms for the prediction of visits to emergency departments by older community-dwelling individuals receiving home care assistance: a proof of concept study. PLoS ONE 14(8), (2019)

Chu, W., Hu, D., Song, G., Kong, X., Wu, Y.: Investigation and analysis of the demands of the elderly and their influencing factors. Chin. Health Serv. Manag. (12), 836–838 (2007). CNKI:SUN:ZWSG.0.2007-12-019

Xu, Q., Chow, J.C.: Exploring the community-based service delivery model: elderly care in China. Int Soc Work 54(3), 374–387 (2011)

Zhao, Y., et al.: Demand and signing of general practitioner contract service among the urban elderly: a population-based analysis in Zhejiang Province, China. Int. J. Environ. Res. Public Health 14(4), 356 (2017)

Yuan, Y., et al.: Demand analysis of telenursing for community-dwelling empty-nest elderly based on the Kano model. Telemed. E-Health, 414–421 (2020). https://doi.org/10.1089/tmj.2020.0037

The Utilization of Online Medical Resources and the Influencing Factors

Hui Wei[1], Ruixue Fang[1], Tingting Zhang[1(✉)], and William Yu Chung Wang[2]

[1] School of Economics and Management, University of Science and Technology Beijing, 30 Xueyuan Road, Beijing 100083, China
tzhang@ustb.edu.cn
[2] Waikato Management School, University of Waikato, Hamilton 3210, New Zealand

Abstract. The effective allocation of online medical resources plays a key role in the popularization and application of online healthcare. However, the existing research has not yet comprehensively and deeply analyzed the online medical resource allocation mechanism. Using data from an online medical platform and regional statistical data, this study to analyze the utilization pattern of online medical resources and identify the influencing factors. It is found that most patients tend to choose doctors from areas with high-quality resource and that the high-quality health resources in some provinces have not been effectively utilized. In addition, doctors from provinces with higher level of economic development, more high-quality health resources and more total number of patients who checked in after consultation are more likely to attract patients on the online health platform. Moreover, when patients chose online consultation, they paid much attention to the technical level of doctors and the number of patients who report after consultation on the platform. The theoretical and practical implications of this study are discussed based on the findings.

Keywords: Online medical resource · Resources utilization · Social network analysis

1 Introduction

With the improvement of economic level, people's health awareness gradually increased. Under the background of medical resource shortage, with the help of the fast-growing Internet and information and communication technology, more and more people have access to medical services through the Internet. The effective operation of online medical service market needs the active participation of doctors, patients and online medical service platform. The effective use of online medical service resources is related to the success of online medical service delivery. Doctors expect to provide services within their expertise to patients in need via an online health service platform, while patients are looking for doctors who can meet their medical needs [1]. However, the expansion of the market size in the online platform tends to increase the search cost of the platform users, thereby reducing the efficiency of the platform's service resource allocation [2].

© Springer Nature Singapore Pte Ltd. 2021
Y. Wang et al. (Eds.): DHA 2020, CCIS 1412, pp. 66–74, 2021.
https://doi.org/10.1007/978-981-16-3631-8_7

Therefore, improving the efficiency of the allocation of online medical service resources is a core work of online medical service platform management.

Online medical services can improve the accessibility of medical services in remote areas, reduce costs, and to a certain extent, alleviate the uneven distribution of offline medical resources [3, 4]. In both developed and developing countries, online health service platforms have reduced medical disparities between rural and urban areas [5, 6]. Such studies mainly focus on the optimization of offline medical resources by online platforms [3]. However, little attention has been paid on the allocation of online medical service resources, especially the underutilization of online high-quality medical resources formed by offline medical resources in underdeveloped areas [7, 8]. In addition, there is a call for corresponding optimization strategy of online medical service resource allocation [9]. Therefore, this study tends to investigate the utilization of online medical service resources and the influential factors.

2 Analysis of the Utilization of Online Medical Resources

2.1 Data Description

The online medical platform provides a combination of online and offline diagnosis and treatment, which is beneficial for doctors to become familiar with patients and for the long-term physical management of patients with chronic diseases. Therefore, this study selects one of the common chronic diseases - coronary heart disease as the object, collect ingress with relevant data.

The data used in this study were collected from the two sources. First, data related to online medical resource, online consultation, and doctors' details were collected from Haodf.com (http://www.haodf.com/). The dataset consists of 2320 recommended hospitals with coronary heart disease department, 4516 recommended doctors specialized in coronary heart disease, 6923 consultation data and 1012 doctors' detailed data. Second, social-economic data for each Chinese province, including GDP, population size and geographical area, were collected from the china statistical yearbook.

2.2 The Distribution of Online Medical Service Resources

Because online medical services are designed to provide patients with better quality medical resources, the emphasis of this study is placed on quantifying quality online medical resources which are divided into two main aspects: high-quality hospital resources and high-quality doctor resources. The volume of high-quality hospital resources in province x (hospital$_x$) is calculated using formula (1), where $L1$–$L7$ represents the grade of a hospital with $L1$ being the lowest grade and $L7$ the highest. Similarly, the volume of high-quality doctor resources in prince x (doctor$_x$) is calculated using formula (2), where $N1$–$N4$ represents the grade of a doctor with $N1$ being the lowest grade and $N4$ the highest.

$$\text{hospital}_x = 1 \times L_1 + 2 \times L_2 + 3 \times L_3 + 4 \times L_4 + 5 \times L_5 + 6 \times L_6 + 7 \times L_7 \quad (1)$$

$$\text{doctor}_x = 1 \times N_1 + 2 \times N_2 + 3 \times N_3 + 4 \times N_4 \quad (2)$$

Table 1. Volume and HRDI of online health resources in each province.

Provinces	Volume of high-quality hospital resources	HRDI of high-quality hospital resources	Volume of High-quality doctor resources	HRDI of high-quality doctor resources
Beijing	770	4.0313	3479	18.2142
Shanghai	481	3.8846	1772	14.3107
Tianjin	244	1.8396	475	3.5812
Shandong	1267	1.0109	1119	0.8928
Jiangsu	857	0.9442	797	0.8781
Zhejiang	711	0.9369	560	0.7379
Liaoning	639	0.8009	585	0.7332
Guangdong	1071	0.7558	1032	0.7282
Hubei	629	0.6005	692	0.6606
Chongqing	319	0.6342	305	0.6063
Shaanxi	484	0.5448	611	0.6877
Hunan	827	0.6545	613	0.4852
Fujian	361	0.5239	309	0.4484
Hunan	570	0.4729	489	0.4057
Jilin	301	0.4218	324	0.4540
Hebei	667	0.5580	350	0.2928
Shanxi	336	0.4421	280	0.3684
Hainan	92	0.5192	51	0.2878
Anhui	435	0.4655	291	0.3114
Heilongjiang	354	0.2644	566	0.4228
Ningxia	94	0.4418	48	0.2256
Jiangxi	287	0.3268	193	0.2197
Sichuan	663	0.3304	315	0.1570
Guangxi	264	0.2457	87	0.0810
Yunnan	252	0.1832	155	0.1127
Gansu	204	0.1866	75	0.0686
Guizhou	121	0.1523	65	0.0818
Inner Mongolia	213	0.1232	76	0.0439
Xinjiang	303	0.1502	32	0.0159
Qinghai	65	0.0990	0	0.0000
Tibet	14	0.0218	0	0.0000

In order to reflect how the population and geographical area affect the per capita density of medical resources, the Health Resource Density Index (HRDI) [10] is calculated using formula (3).

$$HRDI = \sqrt{\frac{volume\ of\ medical\ resources}{population} \times \frac{volume\ of\ medical\ resources}{geographic\ area}} \tag{3}$$

The indicators of quality medical resources in each province are shown in Table 1. Overall, Beijing, Shanghai and Tianjin perform better than other provinces in terms of high-quality hospital resources and high-quality doctor resources. Beijing has the most high-quality medical resources, with its high-quality hospital resources and high-quality doctor resources being as high as 4.0313 and 18.2142, respectively, while Xinjiang, Inner Mongolia, Qinghai and Tibet and other provinces are scarce in quality medical resources.

In order to further explore the regional distribution characteristics of online high-quality medical resources, this study conducts Z-score standardized processing and cluster analysis of HRDI values of high-quality hospital resources and HRDI values of high-quality doctor resources in each province. As shown in Table 2, Beijing and Shanghai have the most high-quality medical resources, followed by Tianjin, Zhejiang, Jiangsu, Shandong, Liaoning and other provinces, Tibet, Qinghai, Inner Mongolia, Xinjiang and other provinces are relatively scarce of high-quality medical resources. It can be seen that the distribution of high-quality medical resources on the online medical platform is about the same as that of offline, mainly concentrated in developed areas.

Table 2. Clustering results of high-quality health resources in each province.

Category	Province
The first category	Beijing, Shanghai
The second category	Tianjin
	Shandong, Jiangsu, Zhejiang
	Liaoning, Guangdong, Hubei, Chongqing, Shaanxi, Henan
	Hebei, Hainan, Fujian, Shanxi, Anhui, Hunan, Jilin, Ningxia
The third category	Guangxi, Heilongjiang, Jiangxi, Sichuan, Tibet, Qinghai, Inner Mongolia, Gansu, Yunnan, Xinjiang, Guizhou

2.3 The Flow of Online Medical Resources

This study adopted social network analysis to explore the structure and attribute characteristics of the flow of online medical resource. In this study, 31 provinces and autonomous regions were treated as nodes. The number of patients in province x who consult a doctor from another province is measured as Outdegree of a node (O_x), while the number of patients in another province who consult a doctor from province x is

Table 3. Settlement results of social network analysis indicators of each province.

Province	Indegree	Outdegree	Total number of patients	Outgoing remote consultation rate	Incoming remote consultation rate	NSI
Beijing	2538	70	703	9.96%	53.92%	0.95
Tianjin	520	40	262	15.27%	8.44%	0.86
Shaanxi	555	62	365	16.99%	7.14%	0.80
Shanghai	326	52	169	30.77%	5.92%	0.72
Guangdong	512	127	389	32.65%	7.08%	0.60
Hunan	200	78	213	36.62%	1.79%	0.44
Jiangsu	431	220	424	51.89%	6.43%	0.32
Sichuan	96	62	136	45.59%	0.60%	0.22
Hubei	180	127	282	45.04%	0.71%	0.17
Guangxi	56	41	85	48.24%	0.34%	0.15
Liaoning	289	222	432	51.39%	2.24%	0.13
Henan	252	194	423	45.86%	0.62%	0.13
Chongqing	45	43	82	52.44%	0.14%	0.02
Yunnan	49	47	83	56.63%	0.37%	0.02
Qinghai	10	10	20	50.00%	0.00%	0.00
Guizhou	33	39	72	54.17%	0.00%	−0.08
Shandong	251	351	591	59.39%	0.31%	−0.17
Jiangxi	39	56	95	58.95%	0.00%	−0.18
Hebei	249	440	665	66.17%	0.68%	−0.28
Zhejiang	60	125	178	70.22%	0.20%	−0.35
Shanxi	79	185	230	80.43%	0.96%	−0.40
Gansu	48	115	128	89.84%	0.99%	−0.41
Hainan	4	15	16	93.75%	0.09%	−0.58
Xinjiang	10	46	55	83.64%	0.03%	−0.64
Fujian	12	66	77	85.71%	0.03%	−0.69
Anhui	28	170	197	86.29%	0.00%	−0.72
Inner Mongolia	31	213	224	95.09%	0.57%	−0.75
Heilongjiang	14	179	188	95.21%	0.14%	−0.85
Jilin	5	103	106	97.17%	0.06%	−0.91
Ningxia	0	30	30	100.00%	0.00%	−1.00

(*continued*)

Table 3. (*continued*)

Province	Indegree	Outdegree	Total number of patients	Outgoing remote consultation rate	Incoming remote consultation rate	NSI
Tibet	0	1	1	100.00%	0.00%	−1.00

measured as Indegree of a node (I_x). In addition, to describe the inflow and outflow differences between provinces, the Node Symmetry Index (Node Symmetry Index, NSI) is introduced, and the formula is calculated as Eq. 4. Where ix is the entry of node x and Ox is the out of node x. If NSI is 0, the inflow of the province is greater than the outflow, and if NSI 0 is, the province's outflow is greater than the outflow. The results of the social network analysis are shown in Table 3.

$$NSI_x = \frac{\sum I_x - \sum O_x}{\sum I_x + \sum O_x} \tag{4}$$

As can be seen from Table 3, Beijing provides medical services for the majority of patients and holds an important position in the online medical community network. However, the high-quality online medical resources in Zhejiang and Shandong are not fully utilized. Further analysis of doctor data found that, the top 100 doctors recommended by coronary heart disease were visited by an average of 1161 times a day with the average total number of patients received being 3046. On the contrary, the average number of visits by 900 to 1000 doctors was 122 visits per day and the average total number of patient visits only 470. Therefore, on the online medical platform, patients mainly flow to Beijing, tend to choose famous doctors, there are less well-known doctors, some provinces of low utilization of medical resources phenomenon.

3 Analysis of the Impact Factors of the Use of Online Medical Resources

Previous studies have found that the number of thank-you letters, the number of heart gifts, and the number of patients reported after diagnosis have a significant positive effect on patient choice behavior, and that patients' trust is related to the credibility of hospitals and doctors. Therefore, the credibility of hospitals and doctors will also affect patients' medical choice behavior. In addition, GDP affects the size of Internet users in each province, which may indirectly affect the number of patients in each province who consult with doctors online.

3.1 Factors Influencing Incoming and Outgoing Consultations

The provinces' GDP, the average number of thank-you letters, the average number of gifts, the average number of patients reported after consultation and the HRDI of high-quality hospital resources and the HRDI of high-quality doctor resources were used as the independent variables, and the node symmetry index of each province was used as the dependent variable. A correlation analysis of the variables found that the Pearson correlation coefficients of the average number of thank you letters and the average number of gifts, the average number of patients reported after the total consultation and the average number of gifts, and HRDI of high-quality hospital resources and HRDI of high-quality doctor resources are higher than 0.6. After excluding the average number of gifts and the HRDI of high-quality hospital resources, the regression model was re-established and the regression results are shown in Table 4. As shown in Table 4, at the significant level of 5%, the GDP of each province, the average number of patients reported after general consultation, and the HRDI value of high-quality doctor resources have significant effects on the difference in incoming and outgoing consultations of each province.

Table 4. Coefficients of the factors influencing incoming and outgoing consultations.

	Unstandardized coefficients		Standardized coefficients	t value	Sig.
	B	Std. error	Beta		
Constant	−0.612	0.138		−4.437	0.000
GDP	7.395E−06	0.000	0.338	2.307	0.029
Average number of patients reported after consultation	0.001	0.000	0.338	2.223	0.035
HRDI value of high-quality doctor resources	0.069	0.021	0.492	3.383	0.002
Average number of thank-you letters	0.000	0.004	0.007	0.042	0.967
$R^2 = 0.521$, Adjusted $R^2 = 0.448$					

3.2   Factors Influencing Patient Consultation in Each Province

In order to further examine the influential factors of patient consultation in different provinces, this study takes the degree centrality of a node as the dependent variable and establishes the regression model with the GDP of each province, the number of thank-you letters, the number of gifts, the number of patients reported after the total consultation, the amount of high-quality hospital resources and the amount of high-quality doctor resources. A correlation analysis found that Pearson correlation coefficients between the number of letters, the number of heart gifts, the number of patients reported after the total diagnosis and the amount of high-quality doctor resources are greater than 0.9 and that between the amount of high-quality hospital resources and the province's GDP is also high. After excluding the GDP of each province, the number of thank-you letters, the number of gifts and the amount of high-quality doctor resources, the regression model was re-established and the regression results are shown in Table 5. As shown in Table 5, at the 5% significance level, the number of patients reported after total diagnosis has a significant effect on the number of patient consultations in various provinces.

Table 5. Coefficients of the factors influencing the patient consultation in each province.

	Unstandardized coefficients		Standardized coefficients	t value	Sig.
	B	Std. Error	Beta		
Constant	1.278	43.818		0.029	0.977
Volume of high-quality hospital resources	0.066	0.087	0.043	0.756	0.456
The number of patients reported after consultation	0.020	0.001	0.942	16.408	0.000
$R^2 = 0.920$, Adjusted $R^2 = 0.915$					

4   Conclusions

This study found that Beijing is the most popular area for patients in the online medical platform, with a high proportion of patients who consulted from different places, and the number of patients served by well-known doctors and other doctors was in obvious contrast, with patients more concentrating on quality medical resources. The results of an analysis of the factors affecting the use of online medical resources showed that patients were more likely to value the doctor's skill level, online word-of-mouth (e.g. number of thank-you letters and the number of gifts) and more likely to choose a doctor who reported a large number after a consultation.

This study enriches the research on resource allocation on the Internet platform with the characteristics of online and offline interaction and provide theoretical and method support for in-depth understanding of the resource allocation mechanism of online medical service resources. In addition, findings from this study suggest several managerial strategies for improving the efficacy of online medical resources allocation. First, online medical platforms should improve the doctor recommendation mechanism by considering the geographical location of patients. Second, online medical platforms should improve the feedback mechanism by encouraging patients to make realistic evaluation of doctors. Third, online medical platforms should guide patients to report after consolation. However, this study used data related to only one type of diseases on a single online medical platform. Further studies may use data from multiple diseases and platforms to further generalized the findings.

Acknowledgement. This research is supported by the Humanity and Social Science foundation of Ministry of Education for Young Scholars (Grant No. 20YJC630214) and the Fundamental Research Funds for the Central Universities (Grant No. FRF-TP-20-022A1).

References

1. Yang, G., Wang, P., Rao, S., Yu, J., Huang, L.: Association between doctor selection habit and precision search on Internet medical platform. Chin. J. Med. Libr. Inf. Sci. **26**(10), 3–33, 49 (2017)
2. Li, J., Netessine, S.: Higher market thickness reduces matching rate in online platforms: evidence from a quasiexperiment. Manag. Sci. **66**(1), 271–289 (2020)
3. Wu, J., Zhou, L.: The trans-reginal flow of medical information resource: The study of online health communities' role in optimizing allocation of medical resource. J. Inf. Resour. Manag. **7**(04), 58–65, 85 (2017)
4. Srivastava, S.C., Shainesh, G.: Bridging the service divide through digitally enabled service innovations: evidence from Indian healthcare service providers. MIS Q. **39**(1), 245–267 (2015)
5. Goh, J.M., Gao, G., Agarwal, R.: The creation of social value: can an online health community reduce rural–urban health disparities? MIS Q. **40**(1), 247–263 (2016)
6. Cao, X., Wang, D.: The role of online communities in reducing urban–rural health disparities in China. J. Assoc. Inf. Sci. Technol. **69**(7), 890–899 (2018)
7. Li, Y., et al.: Exploring the role of online health community information in patients' decisions to switch from online to offline medical services. Int. J. Med. Inform. **130**, (2019)
8. Khurana, S., Qiu, L., Kumar, S.: When a doctor knows, it shows: an empirical analysis of doctors' responses in a Q&A forum of an online healthcare portal. Inf. Syst. Res. **30**(3), 872–891 (2019)
9. Godager, G.: Birds of a feather flock together: a study of doctor–patient matching. J. Health Econ. **31**, 296–305 (2012)
10. Fang, Y., Si, L., Zheng, X., Li, M., Liu, S., Zhang, R.: Study on the health resource density index. Chin. Health Manag. **4**, 253–254 (2000)

The Adoption of Artificial Intelligence in the E-Commerce Trade of Healthcare Industry

Yan Kong[1], Yilin Hou[2], and Shiwei Sun[2(✉)]

[1] School of Economics and Trade, Xinhua College of Sun Yat-sen University (Dongguan), Guangzhou, China
[2] School of Economics and Management, Beijing Institute of Technology, Beijing 100081, China
shiweisun@bit.edu.cn

Abstract. The increasing digital and emerging technologies have changed the value creation of traditional industrial chain to a great extent, and also affected the transaction mode between enterprises. The combination of AI and B2B supply chain has been accepted and adopted by medical field to improve supply-chain efficiency as well as automated e-procurement, or electronic B2B (business-to-business) trade, resulting in significant financial benefits for firms. However, although the e-commerce model of health care industry has brought significant benefits to enterprises and customers, the B2B industry supply chain system of health care industry does not use artificial intelligence as other fields, such as B2C medical field. In our research, intention to adoption an innovation is driven by many factors including transparency of the data, cost pressure, relative advantages, legal regulation. Therefore, one of the contributions of this paper is to fill the gap in the adoption of toe framework related literature in the field of B2B medical model. We also use 'technology-push' (TP) and 'need-pull' (NP) concepts to examine the potential factors that impact the adoption of artificial intelligence in healthcare industry. How we tackle issues from AI intention to implementation will be probably have great impacts for the future practice of AI in B2B industry.

Keywords: Artificial intelligence · Healthcare · Electronic B2B trade

1 Introduction

The emergence of artificial intelligence (AI) and growing interest will have a greater and greater social impact on decision makers. Healthcare organizations, for example, the B2B business between pharmaceutical factories. At the same time, the value creation of B2B has changed with the improvement of digitization and the emergence of new information and communication technologies (Paschen 2019; Wang et al. 2018; Wang et al. 2019). To put it more sharply, great changes have taken place in trade mode because the revolution in terms of how firms manage and use data and knowledge has entered a new era (Gupta et al. 2017).

© Springer Nature Singapore Pte Ltd. 2021
Y. Wang et al. (Eds.): DHA 2020, CCIS 1412, pp. 75–88, 2021.
https://doi.org/10.1007/978-981-16-3631-8_8

In recent years, the combination of AI and B2B supply chain has been accepted and adopted by medical field. And fortunately, the burgeoning strategy of utilizing business to business commerce mode with the help of AI enhances traditional supply-chain efficiency, contributing to significant financial benefits for companies.

The importance and intensity of competition between supply chains has gradually exceeded the competition among individual enterprises due to the rapid development of technology. The healthcare procurement market amounts to dominate manufacturer factor, which increases the possibility of profit by reducing the cost of the medical supply market. Also, it has the potential to bring effective and efficient support to the business activities of the healthcare industry. In fact, as there are increasingly number of companies trying to gain a competitive advantage, e-procurement is a wise strategy to choose (Smith and Flanegin 2004).

Nowadays, one of the important parts of the economy is the healthcare industry. It is a common practice in medical industry to implement e-commerce system in supply chain (Smith and Correa 2005). This is because there are numerable benefits to adopt this new practice (Cullen and Taylor 2009). Healthcare industry is nearly compelled to adjust itself to the application of e-commerce strategy owing to its scale, low efficiency of current paper system and urgent demand for the latest information (Holmes and Miller 2003).

Obviously, people have high expectations for the advantages that e-commerce model could bring to us, which also leads to the increase of expenditure of B2B e-commerce in the medical industry (Wang et al. 2016). However, practitioners and many scholars still know little about its use. Actually, for a long period of time, the lack of cooperation among different parts of the medical supply chain has been considered as the main obstacle to the implementation of cost-benefit standardization process in the medical industry (Nachtmann and Pohl 2009).

Assessing the willingness of a certain company to accept an emerging innovation is a vital prerequisite in today's ever-changing environment (Aboelmaged 2014; Cao et al. 2020). This paper seeks to propose a research framework for the adoption of AI in the B2B healthcare industry. To do so, we will use the Technology- Organizations- Environment (TOE) framework and the technology-push (TP) and need-pull (NP) concepts. In view of the scope of change brought by the penetration of B2B e-commerce in the supply chain, the gap in the use of supply chain in the medical field, substantial benefits can be gained from this kind of research.

In our research, intention to adoption an innovation is driven by many factors including transparency of the data, cost pressure, relative advantages, legal regulation (Liu et al. 2011; Ordanini 2001). Online B2B marketplaces reduces transaction costs as well as the costs of search and negotiation, cut the fat out of inventory and overhead costs (Zhu 2002). Companies adoption e-procurement using AI system can obtain competitive advantages against traditional firms. Furthermore, the environmental regulation functions as catalyzer that can promote the profitability and development of the company.

Nowadays, AI is already being applied much endeavors in healthcare and there have been significant reports of artificial intelligence applications in patients' level. However, in the field of B2B or firm level, the importance of AI adoption has been neglected for a long period.

Therefore, one of the contributions of this paper is to fill the gap in the adoption of toe framework related literature in the field of B2B medical model and the 'technology-push' (TP) and 'need-pull' (NP) concepts, to examine the potential factors that influence the adoption of artificial intelligence in healthcare industry. How we tackle issues from AI intention to implementation will be probably have great impacts for the future practice of AI in B2B industry.

2 Literature Review

2.1 Definition of AI and B2B Supply Chain

There is no unified definition for AI. It is often referred to as the machine's ability to learn from experience, adapt to new inputs, and have the same ability to process information as natural person (Yanqing 2019). These days, artificial intelligence is changing the traditional business model, especially in the top enterprises (Bean 2018). The online B2B market is defined as an infrastructure that creates an Internet connected trading community and provides a mechanism for business-to-business interaction using common standards and computer systems that can be applied to the whole industry (Zhu 2002).

B2B in supply chain management has been widely concerned because of its outstanding performance. Internet and other B2B e-commerce mechanisms can create value for patients and companies by realizing the integration and management of internal and cross enterprise business processes.

2.2 The Technology-Push and Need-Pull (TP-NP) Concepts

Schon (1967) introduced the TP-NP concept as the potential force to bring forth innovations. (Chidamber and Kon 1994). Some scholars (e.g., Zmud 1984) suggested interpreting the behavior to adopt new technology based on the literature related to engineering literature, and thus, introduced TP-NP concept in this area. We need to measure the driving force of new technology in two ways: In terms of the supply side, knowledge and existing technological opportunities are fundamental for the innovation activity of every company; In terms of the demand side, market demand is the other driving force for the introduction of new things (Triebswetter and Wackerbauer 2008).

2.2.1 The Influence of TP Driving Factors on AI Adoption Decision

Relative Advantage. Relative advantage refers to the perceived benefits, which refer to the extent to which AI is better than other competitive technologies and traditional methods of adopting AI at the enterprise level (Zahi 2010). According to some scholars (e.g. Carneiro 2000), comparative advantages are produced by the use of knowledge development potential and the decision-making of knowledge development. It seems like the relative advantage to adopt AI in healthcare industry can overweigh much hinders that prevent adoption when we considering the evolution influence caused by AI.

In the subjective prospective, research shows that consumers are not willing to rely on algorithms to perform tasks that are usually performed by human beings, despite the fact that relying on artificial intelligence can often complete tasks faster and better. (Castelo 2019). We assume that the top managers of pharmaceutical products company will have the same concern when evaluating the adoption of artificial intelligence. Optimism and innovativeness are the enablers of technology readiness in healthcare industry, whereas discomfort and insecurity are inhibitors. But we still allege that the relative advantage of artificial intelligence functions as a booster that encourages its adoption.

Transparency. We concern about the great change of trading environment after deploying B2B electronic marketplaces. In traditional physical market, the transparency of the data is not high and therefore the phenomenon of information asymmetry is very common. The data here mainly refers to medical activities, such as the price of drugs, the number of medical devices, etc. The data may include the quantity of drugs purchased, the daily demand of medical equipment, etc. In the electronic market, information transparency has become a key feature. That is to say, the data is real-time, more transparent, shareable and more synchronous.

Data transparency is not perfect or acceptable. In fact, completely transparent data is good for some companies, but harmful for others (Zhu 2002), which is completely a double-edged sword. Researchers found that information disclosure rules crucially affect the firms' incentives to adopt the new innovations. In particular, B2B E-exchange based on artificial intelligence system provides a relatively transparent online platform, on which information is shared and used among participating companies. And therefore, the attributes of data become transparent instead of opaque.

2.2.2 The Influence of NP Pull Factors on AI Adoption Decision

Cost. When we consider the demand side, we cannot find a factor that makes enterprises eager to adopt e-commerce system because the traditional system can satisfy their requirement basically. On the contrary, the cost pressure, which decrease the need-pull degree, should never be neglected. Because enterprises are not operating in a fully competitive market, if the input price rises or the output price falls, the cost pressure will increase.

Literature shows that hospitals are faced with cost pressure, either control costs, or seek other sources of income according to the source of capital pressure (Hadley et al. 1996). However, in the medical industry, the effective use of B2B e-commerce may directly or indirectly reduce the procurement costs and supply chain costs, and eventually lead to the reduction of medical costs. Therefore, whether e-commerce can really save costs needs further consideration. But it is certain that the adoption of artificial intelligence will bring great pressure to enterprises, especially some small enterprises, which will become an obstacle for enterprises to adopt.

2.3 Technology- Organizational- Environmental (TOE) Framework

In recent decades, there are a few studies on adoption of innovations using different traditional adoption frameworks, (e.g. Awa and Ojiabo 2016; Wu 2011). To some extent, in the field of technology, TAM (Technology Acceptance Model) is more widely used to explain much of the variance in users' behavioral intention. However, we still use TOE model instead because from the perspective of a company, we have to include more variables into our framework besides those variables relative to technology, including perceived ease of use, etc. When we evaluate the potential factors in B2C context, TAM will be one decent choice. Tornatzky and Fleischer developed TOE framework in 1990. TOE refers to technology-organizational- environmental, which is intended to examine firm-level adoption of new products and services.

Government Regulation. According to the classical school, competition, analogous to gravity in physics, was understood as a regulating force in the economy (Luthra et al. 2016).

Government policies or regulations have been recognized as one of the factors that enterprises need to consider (Hung 2014). Through a decade of research, the results show that regulation is the most important stimulus to innovation (Green 2005). Therefore, we add environmental regulation to the factors that can influence the adoption of AI in healthcare industry.

The government's attitude towards emerging technologies, including subsidies, support and opposition, is of great significance to the development of this technology. Because the government's attitude is reflected in the cost of enterprise production, in this study, it is reflected in the cost of supply chain use. If the government can subsidize the use of artificial intelligence, more enterprises will adopt the technology.

Competitive Pressures. Researchers discuss the changes in competitiveness of industrial organizations driven by environmental regulations (Porter and Van der Linde 1995). Organizations try to gain more market share, or human asset management through competition from competing organizations (Lippert and Davis 2006). When other competitors benefit from a new model or system, more companies will feel the pressure, prompting them to imitate the experience of successful companies. Therefore, we believe that pressure from peers may lead to acceptance of new technologies.

Absorptive Capacity. Absorptive capacity of an enterprise is the embodiment of its willingness to invest in absorptive capacity. Specifically, it refers to the ability of an enterprise to recognize the value of new external information, absorb information and apply it to business purposes (Cohen and Levinthal 1990). A large number of literatures point out that the technical achievements of a company play an important role in forming its capacity to use new knowledge. In other words, we can define absorptive capacity as the efficiency of the enterprise relative to the deployed resources (Narasimhan et al. 2006).

We summarize the main independent variables included in our proposed research model and their supporting literature (Table 1).

Table 1. Key variables and supporting literature

Main independent variables	Supporting literature
Relative advantage	Zahi (2010), Aboelmaged (2014), Kumar et al. (2016), Hung (2016), Ifinedo (2005), Zhai (2015), Yang (2015); Jianxing He (2019)
Cost pressure	Ate et al. (2011), Ehrgott et al. 2011, (Hadley et al. 1996), Dai and Kauffman (2003)
Transparency	Zhu (2002), Francisco and Swanson (2018), Hsu et al., Ingrams (2017), Janssen et al. (2012), Pinsker et al. (2008); Xu et al. (2004)
Governmental regulation	Green (2005), Chang and Liu (2006), NDRC and SCIO (2007), Jin et al. (2008), CMIC (2012), Kauffman and Mohtadi (2004)
Top management support	Swink (2000), Castelo (2019), García-Sánchez (2019)
Competitive pressures	Premkumar et al. (1997), Scott (2013), Porter and Van der Linde (1995), (Hadley et al. 1996), Lippert and Davis (2006)

3   Proposition

3.1   TP-NP Concept Proposal

Based on the TP-NP concept, variables relevant to the AI adoption intention are selected to propose a conceptual framework as follows (Fig. 1).

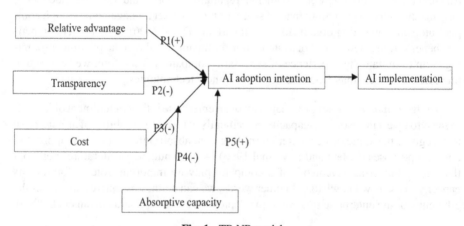

Fig. 1. TP-NP model

Research (e.g. Kumar et al. 2016) found a positive relationship between the relative advantage of new technology and the intention to adopt of an innovation. In this case, the more advantage the managers can realize, the more willingness they will put into the adoption process.

P1: Relative advantage has positive influences on the AI adoption intention.

Data transparency can help some companies obtain necessary information, but it also has a negative impact (Wang et al. 2020; Zhu 2002). In the field of management information system, transparency focuses on the real-time of science and technology, but in practical application, this property is likely to become a hidden danger for participants. The information disclosure of other companies and the risk of information leakage of their own companies will have an impact on the adoption of new technologies. At present, the impact of transparency is still relatively vague. We cannot clearly tell whether it will increase the willingness to adoption or expose the risks of current inventory status and financial status of pharmaceutical companies due to leaked messages. But after all, we assume the negative influence in view of the current situation that artificial intelligence is rarely used in medical field.

P2: Transparency has negative influences on the AI adoption intention.

From the perspective of economics, the role of price is self-evident. Different from figuring out the impactors at the individual level, we are currently focusing on the future development of enterprises. Perhaps individuals will pay attention to psychological factors such as health and happiness, which are often difficult to quantify, and sometimes they can sacrifice money in order to achieve satisfaction. However, enterprises are totally different. As mentioned before, even if AI can provide many conveniences, its inevitable high cost will make many companies shy away (Dai and Kauffman 2003). The purpose of the enterprise is to make profits. Rising costs will directly affect the ultimate interests of enterprises. In other words, even if pharmaceutical companies fully understand the advantages of artificial intelligence in all aspects, as long as the advantages are not higher than or significantly higher than, the cost increase caused by the transformation mode, then the enterprises will not have enough incentive to alter the status quo.

P3: Cost pressure have negative influence on the AI adoption intention.

According to some scholars (Horbach 2008; Kesidou and Demirel 2012), to enhance the absorptive capacity of company requires much effort, including training and information collection, to boost the intent to create something new based on current situation (Díaz-García et al. 2015). Absorptive capacity varies greatly in different companies, and therefore determines that the steps of different companies are different when adopting artificial intelligence. All the procedures will be accompanied by the cost of money. If the company itself has a strong ability to accept new things, such as a complete e-commerce system or other information management systems, then the use of artificial intelligence in supply chain management will not cause great cost.

P4: Absorptive capacity has negative influences on the cost pressure.

Nowadays, the markets is so turbulent and the competition is so fierce that today's information or technology will quickly become obsolete and even be discarded by the market. Due to the constant change of environmental change rate, the strategy of enterprises must be changed accordingly, which is also the research content of many scholars in the past (e.g. Pasa and Shugan 1996). So, the efficiency with which a certain company absorbs know-how from external market can be a decisive factor for the survival and development of the company.

According to some researchers (e.g. Narasimhan et al. 2006), operation capability is one of the factors causing heterogeneity in absorptive capacity (Wang and Byrd 2017). If the absorptive capacity of the enterprise is stronger, then its reliability and quality of using new technology can be more guaranteed (Nath et al. 2010), so that the overall business process of the enterprise will be smooth. In this case, we can draw the good operation ability will lead to good absorptive capacity, which can reduce the cost pressure and promote the adoption of new technology.

P5: Absorptive capacity has positive influences on the AI adoption intention.

3.2 TOE Framework -Hypotheses

We have illustrated the factors of AI adoption by adopting TP-NP concept. Yet, there are some variables that can be considered from the TOE framework. TP-NP concept just explains the demand side from requirement or "need" stand, which is crucial but not exclusive. After including other perspectives, we propose the following hypotheses framework. In addition to TP-NP concept, we add organizational and environmental factors into consideration.

The technological context in the TOE framework's comprises the relative advantage and transparency, whereas the organizational characteristics comprises the resources of a firm including intra-firm communication processes, including firm size, and the amount of slack resources (Borgman et al. 2013). In terms of environmental context, we need to consider the impact of external factors on enterprises, and thus, competitive pressures together with governmental regulation are included (Fig. 2).

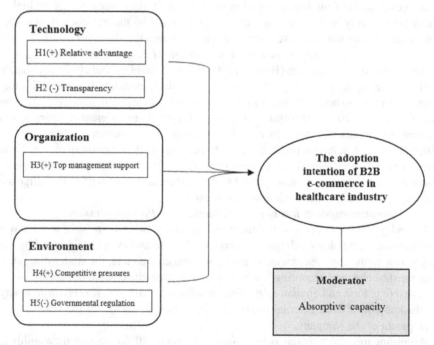

Fig. 2. Conceptual framework based on TOE (adopted from Devis et al. 1986 and Tornatzky et al. 1990)

Relative advantage contributes to the support of top managers to adopt artificial intelligence. However, research has shown that, despite the fact that the quality of AI processing problems is generally better in every form, consumers still don't like to rely on algorithms to perform tasks that are usually performed by natural persons (Castelo 2019). Therefore, further investigation is needed to weigh the degree of support of top managers. However, the managers, as one of the participants who have the ability to implement the adoption behavior, will certainly promote the adoption of AI in the medical field if they support AI.

H3: Top management support has positive influences on the AI adoption intention.

In a competitive environment, organizations need to continuously evaluate the progress of new technologies and adopt them to gain competitive advantage. Therefore, organizations have feedback on external uncertain conditions, which can lead to competitive pressure (Premkumar et al. 1997; Scott 2013). Researchers discuss the changes in competitiveness of industrial organizations driven by environmental regulations (Porter and Van der Linde 1995). Pressure from other competitors generally results from a combination of Government regulation (Hadley et al. 1996). The environment shapes the organizational impact through competition from rival organizations, economic pressures to achieve greater market share, or management of human assets (Lippert and Davis 2006). When other competitors benefit from a new model or system, more companies will feel the pressure, prompting them to imitate the experience of successful companies. Therefore, we believe that pressure from peers may lead to acceptance of new technologies.

H4: Competitive pressures have positive influences on the AI adoption intention.

Despite researchers suggest that government's incentive policy has significant positive effects on corporation's innovation (e.g. Zhao and Sun 2015), most of the relevant policies are about restrictions on the use of artificial intelligence. However, there are many restrictions in the legal regulations. Elon Musk, a scholar from MIT, suggested that it might be a wise choice to conduct some government intervention in view of much uncertainty of artificial intelligence.

The government conducts regulations or even restrictions to artificial intelligence out of various reasons. According to Scherer (2015), the potential of further rapid development of artificial intelligence technology has aroused the concerns of residents, including some calls for legal supervision and restrictions on the operation of artificial intelligence. In particular, in the medical industry, which is closely related to human life, the government will certainly use strict policies to regulate it, and thus, it will have negative influences on the AI adoption intention.

H5: Legal regulation has negative influences on the AI adoption intention.

4 Conclusions and Future Work

Our research has conceptualized the link between the TOE framework and the adoption of artificial intelligence in healthcare industry as well as the moderating effect of absorptive capacity.

The healthcare industry contributes significantly to the economy. For example, Malaysia's healthcare sector accounts for 10% of GDP. When using quantitative indicators to analyze, we can make a good prediction of the country's economic situation, at the same time; we can further improve the living standards of residents. Additionally, our research can help healthcare providers fully understand the needs of e-commerce in healthcare industry. In addition, for whom aiming to adopt artificial intelligence, like some healthcare providers, they can take advantage of supporting variables such as relative advantage, competitive pressures and top management support which then supported electronic commerce usage.

In view of the fact that it is unrealistic to obtain the data of enterprise executives in large quantities in a short period of time, we will gradually carry out a questionnaire survey on the adoption of artificial intelligence by senior leaders of enterprises in the future. The respondents of the questionnaire are concentrated in the medical field. Appendix A presents our scale, which is also the prototype of the questionnaire. In order to ensure the effectiveness of the adjustment variables, we add a technical disturbance to the reserve of the adjustment variables.

Acknowledgement. This research was supported by 2016 Department of Education of Guangdong Province, Key Discipline "Public Administration".

Appendix A. Scale Items

Relative advantage
Please specify the extent to which you agree or disagree with the following statements:
1. Strongly Disagree 2. Somewhat Disagree 3. Neutral 4. Somewhat Agree 5. Strongly Agree

1. An AI system helps us to provide better customer services by giving them quick and latest information about our products and services	1	2	3	4	5
2. An AI system has the ability to provide timely and accurate information for decision-making	1	2	3	4	5
3. An AI system helps generate competitive advantage	1	2	3	4	5
Competitive pressure					
4. Some of our competitors have already started using B2B e-commerce systems	1	2	3	4	5
5. The competition among companies in the industry, which my firm operating in is very tense	1	2	3	4	5
6. Our firm thinks that AI has an influence on competition in our industry	1	2	3	4	5
7. Our firm is under pressure from competitors to adopt AI	1	2	3	4	5
Government support					
8. The local government is helping in giving all kinds of assistance to help to businesses to use AI system in B2B electronic market	1	2	3	4	5
9. The government often inform us about the good points of e-commerce and doing business using the AI systems	1	2	3	4	5
10. Support from government is important to encourage us to use more of AI in business	1	2	3	4	5

(*continued*)

(continued)

11. Government has provided adequate financial assistance to implement and use AI in business	1	2	3	4	5

Cost-effectiveness

12. Initial cost in AI systems relatives to the benefits from AI	1	2	3	4	5
13. The cost and benefit of training enterprises to use AI effectively are related	1	2	3	4	5
14. Costs of integrating new AI systems with other information systems in the firm relative to the benefits from such integration	1	2	3	4	5

AI adoption intention

15. Our company is contemplating to adopt AI in a year's time	1	2	3	4	5
16. Our company is likely to adopt AI in a year's time	1	2	3	4	5
17. Our company is expecting to adopt AI in a year's time	1	2	3	4	5
18. Our company intends to adopt AI with our key business partner in the near future	1	2	3	4	5
19. It is likely that our company will take some steps to adopt AI with our key business partner in the near future	1	2	3	4	5

Dependency

20. Our firm thinks that our business partner is important to our future performance	1	2	3	4	5
21. It would be difficult for us to replace our business partner	1	2	3	4	5
22. We depend on our business partner	1	2	3	4	5

Absorptive capacity

23. Members of our firm have a common language to deal with new practices our organization intends to adopt	1	2	3	4	5
24. Our firm had a vision of what it was trying to achieve through the transfer of new practices	1	2	3	4	5
25. Our firm has the necessary skills to implement the new practices	1	2	3	4	5
26. Our firm has the technical competence to absorb the new practices	1	2	3	4	5

Technological turbulence

27. The technology in our industry is changing rapidly	1	2	3	4	5
28. Technological changes provide big opportunities in our industry	1	2	3	4	5
29. It is very difficult to forecast where the technology in our industry will be in the next two to three years	1	2	3	4	5
30. A large number of new product ideas have been made possible through technological breakthrough in our industry	1	2	3	4	5

Demographics

1. What is your firm size (number of employees)
   (1) 1–500 (2) 500–1000 (3) 1000–2000 (4) 2000+

2. What is industry type of your firm?
   (1) Manufacturing (2) Information Technology (3) Financial Services (4) Construction/Real Estate (5) Retail/wholesale Distribution (6) Public Administration and Social Work (7) Transport, Communication (8) Others
3. What is your job title?
   (1) Top Manager (2) Middle Manager (3) Operations Manager (4) Others
4. What is total revenue of your company?
   (1) About \$1–\$1,000 million (2) About \$1,000–\$10,000 million (3) About \$10,000–\$30,000 million (4) Over \$30,000 million
5. What is your firm age?
   (1) Less than 10 years (2) 11–20 years (3) 21–40 years (4) over 41 years
6. What is the stage of AI implementation in your company?
   (1) Non-adoption (2) Awareness (3) Consideration (4) Intention to adopt (5) Adaptation (6) Infusion

References

Aboelmaged, M.G.: Predicting e-readiness at firm-level: an analysis of technological, organizational and environmental (TOE) effects on e-maintenance readiness in manufacturing firms. Int. J. Inf. Manage. **34**(5), 639–651 (2014)

Aminololama-Shakeri, S., López, J.E.: The doctor-patient relationship with artificial intelligence. Am. J. Roentgenol. **212**(2), 308–310 (2019)

Ateş, M.A., Bloemhof, J., Van Raaij, E.M., Wynstra, F.: Proactive environmental strategy in a supply chain context: the mediating role of investments. Int. J. Prod. Res. **50**(4), 1079–1095 (2012)

Awa, H.O., Ojiabo, O.U.: A model of adoption determinants of ERP within TOE framework. Inf. Technol. People **29**(4), 901–930 (2016)

Bean, R.: How big data and AI are driving business innovation in 2018. MIT Sloan Manag. Rev. (2018)

Borgman, H.P., Bahli, B., Heier, H., Schewski, F.: Cloudrise: exploring cloud computing adoption and governance with the TOE framework. In: 2013 46th Hawaii International Conference on System Sciences, pp. 4425–4435. IEEE (2013)

Cao, D., Tao, H., Wang, Y., Tarhini, A., Xia, S.: Acceptance of automation manufacturing technology in China: an examination of perceived norm and organizational efficacy. Prod. Plan. Control **31**(8), 660–672 (2020)

Carneiro, A.: How does knowledge management influence innovation and competitiveness? J. Knowl. Manag. **4**(2), 87–98 (2000)

Castelo, N.: Blurring the line between human and machine: marketing artificial intelligence (doctoral dissertation). Retrieved from Columbia University Academic Commons (2019). https://doi.org/10.7916/d8-k7vk-0s40

Castelo, N., Bos, M.W., Lehmann, D.R.: Task-dependent algorithm aversion. J. Mark. Res. **56**(5), 809–825 (2019)

Chidamber, S.R., Kon, H.B.: A research retrospective of innovation inception and success: the technology–push, demand–pull question. Int. J. Technol. Manage. **9**(1), 94–112 (1994)

Cohen, W.M., Levinthal, D.A.: Absorptive capacity: a new perspective on learning and innovation. Adm. Sci. Q. **35**, 128–152 (1990)

Cullen, A.J., Taylor, M.: Critical success factors for B2B e-commerce use within the UK NHS pharmaceutical supply chain. Int. J. Oper. Prod. Manag. **29**(11), 1156–1185 (2009)

Dai, Q., Kauffman, R.J.: Understanding B2B e-market alliance strategies. MISRC Work. Pap, 03 (2003)

Díaz-García, C., González-Moreno, Á., Sáez-Martínez, F.J.: Eco-innovation: insights from a literature review. Innovation **17**(1), 6–23 (2015)

Ehrgott, M., Reimann, F., Kaufmann, L., Carter, C.R.: Social sustainability in selecting emerging economy suppliers. J. Bus. Ethics **98**(1), 99–119 (2011)

Graham, G., Hardaker, G.: Supply-chain management across the Internet. Int. J. Phys. Distrib. Logist. Manag. **30**(3/4), 286–295 (2000)

Gupta, S., Keen, M., Shah, A., Verdier, G., Walutowy, M.F.: Digital Revolutions in Public Finance, International Monetary Fund, Washington, DC (2017)

Hadley, J., Zuckerman, S., Iezzoni, L.I.: Financial pressure and competition: changes in hospital efficiency and cost-shifting behavior. Med. Care 205–219 (1996)

Holmes, S.C., Miller, R.H.: The strategic role of e-commerce in the supply chain of the healthcare industry. Int. J. Serv. Technol. Manage. **4**(4–6), 507–517 (2003)

Horbach, J.: Determinants of environmental innovation—new evidence from German panel data sources. Res. Policy **37**(1), 163–173 (2008)

Kauffman, R.J., Mohtadi, H.: Proprietary and open systems adoption in e-procurement: a risk-augmented transaction cost perspective. J. Manag. Inf. Syst. **21**(1), 137–166 (2004)

Kesidou, E., Demirel, P.: On the drivers of eco-innovations: empirical evidence from the UK. Res. Policy **41**(5), 862–870 (2012)

Lippert, S.K., Davis, M.: A conceptual model integrating trust into planned change activities to enhance technology adoption behavior. J. Inf. Sci. **32**(5), 434–448 (2006)

Luthra, S., Garg, D., Haleem, A.: The impacts of critical success factors for implementing green supply chain management towards sustainability: an empirical investigation of Indian automobile industry. J. Clean. Prod. **121**, 142–158 (2016)

Nachtmann, H., Pohl, E.A.: The state of healthcare logistics: cost and quality improvement opportunities. Center for Innovation in Healthcare Logistics, University of Arkansas (2009)

Narasimhan, O., Rajiv, S., Dutta, S.: Absorptive capacity in high-technology markets: the competitive advantage of the haves. Mark. Sci. **25**(5), 510–524 (2006)

Nath, P., Nachiappan, S., Ramanathan, R.: The impact of marketing capability, operations capability and diversification strategy on performance: a resource-based view. Ind. Mark. Manage. **39**(2), 317–329 (2010)

Paschen, J.: Investigating the emotional appeal of fake news using artificial intelligence and human contributions. J. Prod. Brand Manag. **29**(2), 223–233 (2019)

Porter, M., Van der Linde, C.: Green and competitive: ending the stalemate. The dynamics of the eco-efficient economy: environmental regulation and competitive advantage **33** (1995)

Premkumar, G., Ramamurthy, K., Crum, M.: Determinants of EDI adoption in the transportation industry. Eur. J. Inf. Syst. **6**(2), 107–121 (1997)

Scherer, M.U.: Regulating artificial intelligence systems: Risks, challenges, competencies, and strategies. Harv. J. Law Tech. **29**, 353 (2015)

Schon, D.: Technology and Social Change. Delacorte, New York (1967)

Scott, W.R.: Institutions and Organizations: Ideas, Interests, and Identities. Sage Publications, New York (2013)

Smith, A.D., Correa, J.: Value-added benefits of technology. Int. J. Health Care Qual.Assur. **18**(6), 458–473 (2005)

Smith, A.D., Flanegin, F.R.: E-procurement and automatic identification: enhancing supply chain management in the healthcare industry. In. J. Electron. Healthc. **1**(2), 176–198 (2004)

Tornatzky, L.G., Fleischer, M., Chakrabarti, A.K.: Processes of Technological Innovation. Lexington Books, Lanham (1990)

Triebswetter, U., Wackerbauer, J.: Integrated environmental product innovation and impacts on company competitiveness: a case study of the automotive industry in the region of Munich. Eur. Environ. **18**(1), 30–44 (2008)

Wang, Y., Byrd, T.A.: Business analytics-enabled decision-making effectiveness through knowledge absorptive capacity in health care. J. Knowl. Manag. **21**(3), 517–539 (2017)

Wang, Y., Hsiao, S.H., Yang, Z., Hajli, N.: The impact of sellers' social influence on the co-creation of innovation with customers and brand awareness in online communities. Ind. Mark. Manage. **54**, 56–70 (2016)

Wang, Y., Kung, L., Byrd, T.A.: Big data analytics: understanding its capabilities and potential benefits for healthcare organizations. Technol. Forecast. Soc. Chang. **126**, 3–13 (2018)

Wang, Y., Kung, L., Gupta, S., Ozdemir, S.: Leveraging big data analytics to improve quality of care in healthcare organizations: a configurational perspective. Br. J. Manag. **30**(2), 362–388 (2019)

Wang, Y., Xiong, M., Olya, H.: Toward an understanding of responsible artificial intelligence practices. In: Proceedings of the 53rd Hawaii International Conference on System Sciences, pp. 4962–4971 (2020)

Wu, W.W.: Developing an explorative model for SaaS adoption. Expert Syst. Appl. **38**(12), 15057–15064 (2011)

Zhu, K.: Information transparency in electronic marketplaces: why data transparency may hinder the adoption of B2B exchanges. Electron. Mark. **12**(2), 92–99 (2002)

Zmud, R.W.: An examination of "push-pull" theory applied to process innovation in knowledge work. Manag. Sci. **30**(6), 727–738 (1984)

The Effectiveness of the Physician-Patient Relationship Crisis Communication Strategy

Tingting Zhang[✉], Menghui Liu, Xiangbin Yan, and Jiahua Jin

School of Economics and Management, University of Science and Technology Beijing, 30
Xueyuan Road, Beijing 100083, China
tzhang@ustb.edu.cn

Abstract. The widespread use of the Internet provides people with easy access to
information and ways of expressing opinions, which also poses high expectations
to crisis management. In the era of social media, how the hospital can diminish
the public's negative emotion in crisis regarding physician-patient relationship by
applying effective crisis communication strategies has attracted the attention of
both academia and practice. Based on the situational crisis communication theory
and social mediated crisis communication theory, this paper empirically examined
the effectiveness of crisis communication strategies using a real physician-patient
relationship crisis and the public's behavior data. The results reveal that the negative emotion tendency is lower if the crisis event is communicated through the
hospital's official channel, is for the behavior of commenting, and is towards
the hospital. This study contributes to the literature by enhancing the use of the
two aforementioned theories in a healthcare context and to practice by providing
practical suggestions for responding to physician-patient relationship crisis.

Keywords: Physician-Patient relationship · Social media · Public opinion ·
Crisis communication · Sentiment analysis

1 Introduction

The popularization and application of the Internet facilitates people's access to information and expression of wills. As of December 2018, the size of internet users in
China reached 829 million, with 98.6% of them using mobile phones to surf the internet
and instant communication, online news, search engine being used the most, especially
social media usage with 42.3% of the Chinese netizens using Weibo [1]. Social media
has increasingly become a platform for the spread of social opinion, especially involving
events closely related to people's livelihood, which poses challenges for the management
team handle the events.

Healthcare disputes can easily become fierce public opinion on social media because
people are highly concerned with the delivery of healthcare service. In the face of such
public opinion events, if the hospital deals with the issue improperly, the spread of negative public opinion can deepen the conflict between doctors and patients. Such events not
only affect the over healthcare environment and people's choice of healthcare providers,

Y. Wang et al. (Eds.): DHA 2020, CCIS 1412, pp. 89–95, 2021.
https://doi.org/10.1007/978-981-16-3631-8_9

but also affect the reputation and long-term development of the hospital involved. Therefore, in the age of social media, how to effectively weaken the negative emotions of the public is a common concern in academia and practice.

2 Literature Review

Public opinion is a collection of all attitudes, opinions, emotions and behavioral tendencies that are characterized by mass tendencies in a variety of matters that occur in a particular time and space. Online public opinion on the doctor-patient relationship refers to "the cumulation of the cognition, attitude, emotion and behavior tendency towards the doctor-patient relationship and hospital reputation which is stimulated by incidents in a hospital" [2]. Like other types of online public opinion, the evolution process of online public opinion on doctor-patient relationship includes incubation period, outbreak period, spread and diffusion period, and fading and recovery period [3]. Because of the high social attention on doctor-patient relationship, such online public opinion has the characteristics of long incubation period, rapid outbreak and wide participation [2]. Existing research has investigated how to respond to online public opinion on doctor-patient relationship before the occurrence of public opinion events, after the breakout of the crisis [4], and in the fading period of public opinion [5, 6]. These studies suggest that hospitals need to pay attention to the communication strategies while dealing with online public opinion on the doctor-patient relationship.

In the age of social media, the effectiveness of crisis communication depends not only on crisis response strategies, but also on the sources of response information [7]. The public is more receptive to official information published by the organization than by other means [8]. Therefore, facing of online public opinion on the doctor-patient relationship, the hospital should make use of the official channels to make active and timely announcement about the hospital's attitude towards crisis investigation and punishment, disposal progress, to avoid the wide-spread dissemination of false information brought about by suspicion and misunderstanding [3]. The emotional change of public response to online public opinion on the doctor-patient relationship can be an important index to measure the effectiveness of hospital's strategies. The role of emotional tendency in social media crisis communication has been intensively investigated in recent years [9].

Existing research on online public opinion on the doctor-patient relationship mainly focuses on the pattern, the social network structure and its role in the process of its evolution and dissemination. However, research on the management strategies is still in its infancy and lacks of empirical research [2, 4, 5]. Although there are studies on the crisis management of other types of online public opinion, most of them are conducted using situational simulation experiments or questionnaires [8] and little has been done regarding the effectiveness of organizational response strategies for crisis events where responsibility is attributed to ambiguity [10]. Therefore, based on the theory of contextual crisis communication and the theory of social media crisis communication, this paper empirically analyses the effectiveness of hospital response strategy from the perspective of the change of public sentiment. While enriching existing research, this study provides some practical suggestions for hospitals to deal with the crisis of online public opinion on doctor-patient relationship.

3   Theoretical Foundation and Hypotheses Development

People usually look for the cause of an incident to determine the attribution of responsibility and show emotions towards the parties involved according to their responsibility for the occurrence of the incident [11]. Based on this notion, the situational crisis communication theory (SCCT) was proposed [12], which is composed of three elements: crisis situation, crisis response strategy, and matching system of crisis situation and crisis response strategy. This theory explains that crisis responsibility and response strategy affect the emotional response of stakeholders, which further influences the behavioral intention of stakeholders. The public's feelings in crisis events can be well understood by taking an emotional perspective and used to assess the crisis situation for making reasonable communication strategies [13]. In particular, negative emotions have an important impact on the effectiveness of communication in crises. This is because negative feelings about organizations in crisis events not only increase their propensity for negative verbal reporting of the organizations, but also reduce the intention of people to purchase products or services from the them [12]. If people feel angry towards an organization in a crisis event, they tend to choose to express such a feeling and further spread the news that report this event [14]. Features such as "comment" and "forward" on social media can contribute to the development of public opinion crisis events [15]. Therefore, it is hypothesized that:

Hypothesis 1: Forward reflects a sentiment tendency that is stronger than a comment.

Mediated crisis communication theory (SMCC) combines SCCT with the characteristics of social media in the communication of public opinion crisis [8]. SMCC holds that social media information from difference sources perform differently in their roles in a crisis [4]. Because of this, biased media report and the subjective judgment of the media personnel are considered to be the primary cause of the hospital public opinion events and worsening the hospital public opinion crisis [16]. In fact, the public is more receptive to official information published by the organization than by other means [8]. Therefore, it is hypothesized that:

Hypothesis 2: The public shows a stronger sentiment propensity towards news posted by unofficial accounts than that by the official account.

According to SCCT, crisis response strategies and stakeholder responses vary according to the degree to which the organization is accountable to crisis [12]. Therefore, it is necessary to link public emotion with the corresponding subjects' responsibility in the analysis of the public's emotional tendency in online public opinion [17]. Online public opinion on doctor-patient relationship usually involves both the hospitals and patients. However, in such crisis, the hospital side is often considered to be a strong party, while the patient is regarded as a weak party. As a result, the public tend to sympathize with or support patients and their families, while holding resistance and negative feelings towards health care workers [18]. Therefore, it is hypothesized that:

Hypothesis 3: The public is more sentiment inclined to the hospital than to the patient side.

4 Empirical Analysis

4.1 Data Description

On August 31, 2017, a pregnant woman jumped from the 5th floor and died while waiting for production in Yulin First Hospital, Shaanxi province. This woman's family and the hospital both argued that the other party should be responsible for the death. This event became a hot topic on social media, which had 6,052 Weibo entries, 941 pieces of online news, and 313 WeChat articles. This is a typical doctor-patient relationship crisis. During the evolution of the public opinion, the hospital released two official announcements as responds to the views of public opinion, on the September 3 and 6, respectively. In the end, the public opinion of the incident did not develop into blind accusations and cyber violence against the hospital. It was belied that the rational response of hospitals involved plays an important role. Thus, this study is considered a suitable case to investigate the effectiveness of hospital response strategy from the perspective of public emotion.

The application and importance of microblogs in hospital public opinion management has been widely recognized [19]. Especially, the text information in Weibo can be used to extract the views and attitudes of public [20]. This study used all the forwards and comments on the two announcements released by the official Weibo account of Yulin First Hospital and that posted by Today's Headline's Weibo account is a news agent.

4.2 Sentiment Analysis

The sentiment dictionary used in this study was established by integrating open Chinese dictionaries such as HowNet and NTUSD with a dictionary of positive, negative, negative and transition conjunctions which is constructed based on Weibo comments.

The value of a sentiment is calculated using formula (1):

$$s = \sum_{k=0}^{w} p_k + \sum_{j=0}^{m} N_j \begin{cases} s > 0 & \text{positive} \\ s < 0 & \text{negative} \\ \sum_{k=0}^{w} p_k = \sum_{j=0}^{m} N_j = 0 & \text{no sentiment} \\ \text{others} & \text{neutrality} \end{cases} \quad (1)$$

Where, w and m represent the numbers of positive and negative words in each sentence, respectively; p_k is the score of the kth positive word; N_j is the score of the jth negative word.

In order to further distinguish the target of emotional expression, this study classified a target as the hospital when words such as "hospital", "doctor", "physician", "nurse", and "caregiver" appear in the text and as the patients' family when words such as "family", "husband", and "mother" appear. The results of the text sentiment analysis are shown in Table 1.

Table 1. The number of positive and negative comments and forwards

		Hospital's side		Patient's side	
		Positive	Negative	Positive	Negative
First official announcement	Comment	110	924	40	1495
	Forward	13	91	5	481
First non-official announcement	Comment	9	146	11	334
	Forward	0	11	2	223
Second official announcement	Comment	394	4616	370	16073
	Forward	115	2477	186	19807
Second non-official announcement	Comment	136	3071	298	14244
	Forward	10	619	90	7707

4.3 Sentiment Tendency

In this paper, Janis-Fadner (J-F) non-equilibrium coefficient was used to further quantify the degree of sentiment tendency. Janis-Fadner non-equilibrium coefficient is an index proposed by Janis & Fadner for content analysis, which is widely used to measure the tendency of media reporting [21]. It is believed that the Janis-Fadner non-equilibrium coefficient can be used to quantify the degree of positive and negative sentiment tendency of public reaction in crisis communication [22], which can be calculated using formula (2):

$$
J - F \text{ coefficient} = \begin{cases} \dfrac{(e^2 - ec)}{t^2}, & \text{if } e > c \\ \dfrac{(ec - e^2)}{t^2}, & \text{if } e < c \\ 0, & \text{if } e - c \end{cases} \tag{2}
$$

Where, e and c represent the numbers of replies with positive emotion and negative emotion, respectively; t is the sum of e and c. The value of the J-F coefficient ranges from -1 to 1. The greater the number of responses with positive emotions, the closer the value is to 1 and the higher the positive emotional tendency of the public response, and vice versa.

The results of the analysis of the comments on two announcements and the degree of emotional orientation of the forwarded information shown in Table 2. The sentiment tendency of the public is found negative for both the hospital side and the patient side, which is consistent with the findings of the existing study. The main reason is that the medical public opinion involved in the doctor-patient relationship will have a negative impact in the society in general [18].

The results of this paper show that the sentiment tendency of forwards is stronger than that of comments, supporting hypothesis 1. This finding is in align with existing literature which indicates that the negative emotion is more likely to be spread out. In addition, the

Table 2. The sentiment tendency of comments and forwards.

		Hospital's side	Patient's side
First official announcement	Comment	−0.703	−0.923
	Forward	−0.656	−0.969
First non-official announcement	Comment	−0.833	−0.906
	Forward	−1.000	−0.973
Second official announcement	Comment	−0.776	−0.934
	Forward	−0.871	−0.972
Second non-official announcement	Comment	−0.876	−0.939
	Forward	−0.953	−0.966

sentiment tendency in the unofficial channel is found to be stronger than that in the office channel, which supports hypothesis 2. This finding suggests that the hospital should promptly respond on its official social media account after the occurrence of public opinion events, actively reporting the actual situation and development of the crisis events to control the pace of the development of the incident and avoid further damage to the hospital reputation. However, interestingly, the public's sentiment tendency towards the patient side is found stronger than that towards the hospital side, suggests that hypothesis 3 is not supported. Such a finding reflects to a certain extent that the disclosure of the detailed event process helped make the public rational in determining the party who should be responsible for the event.

5   Conclusion

This study examines the effectiveness of the response strategies of the hospital using data from an actual doctor-patient relationship crisis and semantic analysis method. This study contributes to the literature by applying situational crisis communication theory and the social media crisis communication theory in a crisis event where the responsibilities of the involved parties are ambiguous. Results of this study suggest that the hospital should consider releasing the facts regarding the events when a doctor-patient relationship crisis first came out on social media, so that the public can understand the truth in a timely manner to avoid the spread of untruthful opinion. Besides, in the early stage of a doctor-patient relationship crisis, the hospital should pay close attention to the comments and forward published with negative emotional tendencies.

However, this paper only pays attention to the influence of hospital coping strategies on public sentiment during the gestation period and the climax period of the crisis. future research will also consider a hospital's strategies during other periods in the whole cycle of crisis events.

Acknowledgement. This research is supported by the Humanity and Social Science foundation of Ministry of Education for Young Scholars (Grant No. 20YJC630214) and the Fundamental Research Funds for the Central Universities (Grant No. FRF-TP-20-022A1).

References

1. China Internet Network Information Center: The 43rd Statistical report on the Development of Internet in China (2019)
2. Dong, H.: Research on emergency response of hospital emergencies in the new media era. J. Jiangsu Norm. Univ. (Philos. Soc. Sci. Ed.) **44**(02), 85–92 (2018)
3. Huang, H., Piao, Y., Chang, C.: Evaluation of hospital's coping style of public opinion based on the theory of risk communication. Med. Soc. **29**(04), 62–66 (2016)
4. Zhang, M., Liu, X., Xia, Y.: Online public opinion alienation analysis of significant doctor-patient dispute cases. J. Intell. **35**(04), 64–69 (2016)
5. DiStaso, M.W., Vafeiadis, M., Amaral, C.: Managing a health crisis on Facebook: how the response strategies of apology, sympathy, and information influence public relations. Pub. Relat. Rev. **41**(2), 222–231 (2015)
6. Wang, Y., Lv, Y.: Research on strategies taken by hospitals to address crises under the background of Wechat communication. Jiangsu Sci. Technol. Inf. **28**, 67–68 (2016)
7. van Zoonen, W., van der Meer, T.: The importance of source and credibility perception in times of crisis: crisis communication in a socially mediated era. J. Public Relat. Res. **27**(5), 371–388 (2015)
8. Liu, B.F., Austin, L., Jin, Y.: How publics respond to crisis communication strategies: the interplay of information form and source. Public Relat. Rev. **37**(4), 345–353 (2011)
9. Johansen, B.F., Johansen, W., Weckesser, N.M.: Emotional stakeholders as "crisis communicators" in social media: the case of the Telenor customer complaints crisis. Corp. Commun. Int. J. **21**(3), 289–308 (2016)
10. Bentley, J.M., Oostman, K.R., Shah, S.F.A.: We're sorry but it's not our fault: organizational apologies in ambiguous crisis situations. J. Conting. Crisis Manag. **26**(1), 138–149 (2018)
11. Weiner, B.: An attributional theory of achievement motivation and emotion. Psychol. Rev. **92**(4), 548 (1985)
12. Timothy, C.W., Holladay, S.J.: The negative communication dynamic: exploring the impact of stakeholder affect on behavioral intentions. J. Commun. Manag. **11**(4), 300–312 (2007)
13. Jin, Y., Pang, A., Cameron, G.T.: Integrated crisis mapping: toward a publics-based, emotion-driven conceptualization in crisis communication. Sphera Publica (2007)
14. Lee, Y.-C., Wu, W.-L.: Effects of medical disputes on internet communications of negative emotions and negative online word-of-mouth. Psychol. Rep. **117**(1), 251–270 (2015)
15. Zheng, B., Liu, H., Davison, R.M.: Exploring the relationship between corporate reputation and the public's crisis communication on social media. Public Relat. Rev. **44**(1), 56–64 (2018)
16. Zhang, Q.: Research on the hospital crisis responses in the new media era. Henan Med. Res. **26**(08), 1399–1400 (2017)
17. Chen, Y., Zhang, Q.: Analysis on entity relationship of online public opinion information. Inf. Resour. Work **37**(06), 28–34 (2016)
18. Chen, S.: Research on the online opinion of doctor injury events and countermeasures. Acad. Comment (06), 101–106 (2013)
19. Yin, L., et al.: The implementation of content analysis of Weibo crisis in hospital management. J. China-Japan Friendship Hosp. **27**(06), 367-368+370 (2013)
20. Liang, X., et al.: A review on corporate public opinion for social networks. Chin. J. Manag. **14**(06), 925–935 (2017)
21. Shen, H., Feng, J.: Media monitoring, government supervision, and corporate environmental disclosure. Account. Res. **2**, 72-78+97 (2012)
22. Timothy, C.W., Holladay, S.J.: Amazon.com's Orwellian nightmare exploring apology in an online environment. J. Commun. Manag. **16**(3), 280–295 (2012)

The Influence of User Perceived Value of Sports APP on Platform Commodity Purchase

Yidan Liu, Yajun Shen, and Shiwei Sun[✉]

School of Economics and Management, Beijing Institute of Technology, Beijing, China
shiweisun@bit.edu.cn

Abstract. With the improvement of people's living standards, people pay more and more attention to sports health. At the same time, sports health industry has entered a period of vigorous development. In the increasingly popular environment of smart phones, a variety of sports APP brands develop their brand products, and the sales revenue of platform brand products has also become an important part of brand profits.

Based on the perceived value of users of sports APP, this paper selected two dimensions of perceived value, perceived brand and perceived trust, collected data through questionnaire survey, and established a model of the influence of perceived brand, perceived trust and perceived brand and perceived trust on users' purchase behavior. Based on this, some practical Suggestions are provided to the sports APP merchants, with the purpose of improving the commodity purchasing behavior of users on their platform.

Keywords: Sports APP · Perceived value · APP brand product · Purchasing behavior

1 Introduction

1.1 Research Background

In recent years, with the proposal of China's "Healthy China" strategy, the development and popularization of smart phone APP brand platform software, and the development of human body smart device technology, many startups have entered the field of sports and health to develop their strengths and developed many sports and health brand APPs.

Sports APP as a record of people's exercise habits, a tool of providing exercises advice, managing people's exercise behavior and training exercise habits, has great brand value in our lives. For example, advertisements of brand products placed in APP brand platform like "Keep" and "Godong Sports", there are some sports-related products under the brand in the APP mall, there are clothing of the brand, sports auxiliary equipment, smart sportswear, light food, etc. These are all about Sports APP brand's commodity derivatives have certain economic value.

At present, domestic sports and health brand APPs include "Keep", "Godong Sports", "Yue Running Circle", "Huawei Sports Health", and "Xiaomi Sports". Foreign sports

Y. Wang et al. (Eds.): DHA 2020, CCIS 1412, pp. 96–117, 2021.
https://doi.org/10.1007/978-981-16-3631-8_10

APPs include "Fit Bit", "My Fitness Pal" and so on. The Nike brand has also developed related sports health APPs such as "Nike Run Club", "Nike Training".

In the APP brand malls of these sports APPs, modules such as advertisement placement and sales of hardware devices not only affect the behavior of users, but also are an important aspect of achieving revenue. Many sports health APP developed its own brand products, APP has been advertising with the APP sales of branded products and so on. Therefore, the movement of the user to explore the APP perceived value and purchase sports APP relationship brand product behavior, and, accordingly targeted actions, the movement of APP brand products company has a very important significance.

1.2 Review of Related Literature

In the research on the impact of Minghan Huang's sports APP on sports consumption behavior, combined with previous studies, the main factors of perceived value were selected to use the four dimensions of perceived utility, perceived emotion, perceived brand, and perceived trust to evaluate the consumer's perceived value [1]. On this basis, a theoretical model for research was constructed. In their research, the perceived brand and perceived value have higher reliability and validity in the perceived value of sports consumers, and it also fits the focus of the purchase behavior of APP brand products. Therefore, we chose perceived brand and perceived trust as the representative of the APP's perceived value evaluation to study the impact of users' perceived value of the sport APP on purchase behavior.

Chuanhai Liu pointed out that sports APP has a significant role in promoting the user's sports behavior in the study of sports APP for people's physical exercise behavior and habit formation [2]. The survey shows that 80% of users believe that sports APPs can help increase the user's enthusiasm and plan for sports, and have a significant effect on promoting physical exercise behavior and developing physical exercise habits.

Lin Wang, Mengdi Hu, Wenjing Zhu used smart bracelet for users in motion social platform behavior. The study found that the use of sports social platform will affect users of smart bracelet and buy the same, the user in the social platform. The difference in behavior will also affect users' use and purchase of smart bracelets [3].

In Lin Lin's research on the influencing factors of consumer APP mobile shopping behavior, subjective norms which were used to perceive behavior control attitudes, positively influence on intention [4]. The positive influence on behavior have verified the TPB model for explaining and predicting consumption. Customer's own conditions, such as money, the proficiency of using APPs, the cognition operations APP influence the purchase on platform commodity. At the same time, consumers will be influenced by the family and friends around them on the APP mobile shopping experience.

1.3 Research Significance

Researches with regard to APP buying behavior, perceived value, sports APP research related to purchases of goods platform brands can be found on the current academic movement APP research platform brand impact of the purchase, not a lot, there are no sports APP platform merchandise Related research on purchasing behavior. This research mainly aims at the user's perception of the value of sports APP, and analyzes and verifies the purchase behavior of the APP brand products.

Compared with previous articles, we emphasize the APP brand's purchase behavior of sporting goods rather than the general consumer behavior of sports products, and strengthen the APP brand's perceived brand and perceived trust.

2 Theoretical Background

2.1 Sports APP

APP is short for the APP lications, sports health class APP is divided into sports and health monitoring and management classes APP [2].

Health monitoring and management APP, mainly through the connection of body fat scales, blood glucose meters and other equipment to assess body weight or blood glucose physical indicators, you can also monitor continuous heart rate to prevent premature heart fibrillation.

Sports and fitness classes APP main function is to record motion data, for example, in conjunction with the phone GPS function to record, trajectory, recommend related training programs from time speed, user guide scientific training, or a combination of smart wearable device brand to better assess the curriculum effect. For example, a sports APP—"Keep" can connect the Keep bracelet to sense the movement amplitude and monitor the heart rate when participating in the exercise class to adjust the exercise intensity.

Sports fitness APPs can also connect users with other smart devices, such as wristbands to provide users with rhythm and cadence, independent GPS to record the movement track, for the "running elf" sensor on running shoes, which can provide swing amplitude, impact on the ground, and foot landing Regional and other running posture guidance to help users better understand the movement.

As the sports APP is a product of the smartphone era, the young people group has also become the main answerer of the questionnaire. Considering the young people group because of objective conditions, economics and other reasons, the main categories of sports health APPs used are fitness, running, cycling using motion APP purpose is to record the main motion data, generate reports to share sports and so on; therefore referred to herein sports health APP, mainly it refers to have fitness and running APP based.

2.2 Perceived Value

From a marketing sense, it has a value that is obtained using the total cost, the lowest of circumstances, to meet customer demand satisfaction for the consumer sector markets, perceive the same thing is different for different consumers like, and therefore, early in the 20th century, 80 end of the decade, Zeithaml (1998) proposed the "customer perceived value" (the customer perceived, value) concept [5].

The research theory is created from the SOR model of cognitive psychology. The Howard Chase model formally revised in 1969 was derived from the stimulus response theory [6]. The theory is that consumers receive information after receiving product stimuli, social stimuli, and symbol stimuli, and generate various motives to form a series of intermediaries for purchasing decisions. Factors to facilitate purchase results.

3 Research Model

This article takes the people who use sports APP as the survey object.

3.1 Ideas

First, in order to demonstrate that the perceived behavior of sports APP has a positive impact on the purchase behavior of platform brand products, the author conducts research and analysis of relevant literature, finds relevant theoretical basis, and clarifies the purpose and significance of the research.

Secondly, according to the clear research purpose, the research methods and research ideas of the research object, comb the relevant theories, put forward hypothesis design questionnaires and issue them.

Next, make statistics on the valid questionnaires, and use SPSS 26.0 statistical software to verify the validity and validity of the survey data.

3.2 Methods

Literature. This article through reading and researching the literature related to this research, to understand the previous research results, in order to obtain the necessary background materials and theoretical basis, to provide support for the formation of the research argument and model construction.

Interview. This article through in-depth interviews with APP users, to understand the main characteristics of sports APP and consumer experience in the use of sports APP mobile process, so that the scale has a certain scientific and realistic.

Questionnaire. This paper designs the corresponding questionnaire by referring to the relevant research results at home and abroad, combined with the interview results, and after the preliminary survey, the questionnaire content is modified to form the final questionnaire. Obtain the required data by issuing questionnaires online.

Data Statistics. This article uses SPSS 26.0 statistical software to analyze the data, study the correlation between the variables, and draw corresponding conclusions.

3.3 Hypothesis

Through literature review of previous studies, the perceived value is divided into two dimensions: perceived brand and perceived trust, aiming at users' purchase behaviors on sports social platforms. In addition, this study introduces gender as a moderating variable to explore its impact on purchasing behavior. In summary, the following research hypotheses are proposed:

a: Sports APP users perceive that brands have a positive impact on platform product purchase behavior.

b: Perceived trust of sports APP users has a positive effect on the purchase behavior of platform products.

c: Perceived value of sports APP users (perceived brand and perceived trust) has a positive effect on the purchase behavior of platform products.

d: Gender regulates the brand perception of sports APP users on the purchase behavior of platform products.

e: Gender has a moderating effect on the perceived trust of sports APP users on the purchase behavior of platform products.

f: Gender has a moderating effect on the perceived value of sports APP users on the purchase behavior of platform products.

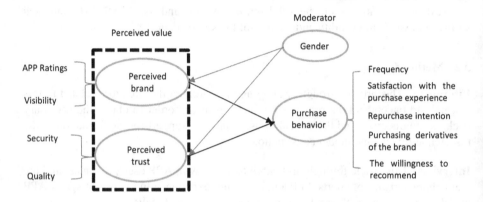

4 Methodology

4.1 Research Design

Questionnaire Design. The questionnaire designed in this article is divided into three parts:

Part I: Basic user information, including gender, age, educational background, and monthly living expenses.

Part II: the perceived value of sports APP users, this part includes perceived brand and perceived trust. The specific content is: the user's tendency to download based on the evaluation, ranking, and fame of the sports APP, and the awareness of the safety, quality, and reputation of the APP.

Part III: Users' purchase behavior of items in the sports APP mall, including research on consumer's basic behavior, satisfaction, repurchase willingness and derivative behavior.

4.2 Variables

In this paper, the perceived value of sports APP users is selected as the independent variable, and the user's purchasing behavior as the dependent variable. For the independent variable measuring points to two parts: the perception of brand trust and perception.
The details are as follow:

Table 1. Variables and specific measurement items

Variable		Specific measurement items	Source
Brand perception (Independent variable)	User perceived value	Q12: I will download sports APP highly rated by others Q13: I think that the top of the sports APP rankings are generally launched by relatively well-known developers Q14: I will give priority to download sports APPs launched by more famous developers	Research on the Influence of Sports APP on Sports Consumption Behavior Minghan Huang [1]
Perceived trust (Independent variable)		Q15: I think sports APPs downloaded via mobile phones are safer Q16: I trust the quality of the sports APP I downloaded Q17: I think the sports APP developers in the APP store are all reputable	
Purchase behaviour (Dependent variable)	Consumer's basic behavior	Q18: How many times have you purchased the most commonly used sports APP platform brand products? (Such as Xiaomi bracelet, keep mall light food, godong mall equipment, etc.) Q19: When was the last time you purchased a brand product of the sports APP platform (reliability is not high due to the epidemic)	Empirical Research on the Effect of Virtual Brand Community Value Perception on Brand Loyalty[7]
	Consumers' willingness to repurchase and satisfaction	Q20: You are satisfied with the experience of purchasing sports APP platform products Q21: If I want to buy such products in the future, I will choose the brand Q22: If necessary, I will buy other products of the brand	
	Consumer derivation	Q23: I will actively recommend this brand to my friends	

4.3 The Distribution and Recovery of Questionnaires

The fill-out the questionnaire in this article are mainly college students, college students have a certain sporting values and the mobile phone APP of active users, in line with the movement APP user perceived value on consumer behavior research topics. A total of 190 valid questionnaires were collected in this questionnaire.

5 Data Analysis

5.1 Data Preprocessing

Check the completeness and accuracy of the data, and remove the blank part of the questionnaire data.

5.2 Descriptive Statistics

Basic information
Statistics for the first part of the questionnaire is to collect basic personal information (Table 2).

The proportion of men and women who filled out the questionnaire was 41.6% and 58.4%, which were close to 1:1, and there was no obvious gender deviation, indicating that the gender ratio of the study subjects was normal.

Table 2. Sampling Profiles

	Value	Frequency	Frequency (%)	Cumulative frequency (%)
Gender	Male	79	41.6%	41.6%
	Female	111	58.4%	100
Age	18 years old and below	8	4.2%	4.2%
	18–25 years old	149	78.4%	82.6%
	25–35 years old	24	12.6%	95.3%
	35–50 years old	7	3.7%	98.9%
	Over 50 years old	2	1.1%	100.0%
Education background	High school and below	9	4.7%	4.7%
	Specialist	13	6.8%	11.6%
	Undergraduate	158	83.2%	94.7%
	Master's degree	10	5.3%	100.0%
	PhD students and above	0	0.0%	100.0%
Monthly living expenses	Below 1,000 yuan	16	8.4%	8.4%
	1000–2000 yuan	94	49.5%	57.9%
	2000–3000 yuan	56	29.5%	87.4%
	More than 3000 yuan	24	12.6%	100.0%

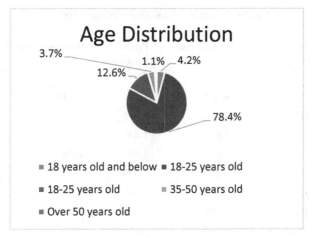

Fig. 1. Age distribution of respondents

The ages of the respondents are mainly between 18–25 years old, accounting for 78.4% (149 people) of the total population, followed by 25–35 years old people, accounting for 12.6% (24 people). More than 90% of users receive or are receiving college-level education, and about 80% of users' monthly living expenses are between 1,000 and 3,000 yuan.

Generally speaking, the entrants are young people and are active users of mobile APPs. And have a good understanding of sports value, in terms of financial level, also have the ability to buy sports social platform products. Contents related to "Sports Social Platform", "Purchasing Behavior", etc. that meet the research of this topic.

Descriptive statistics of each variable
Before conducting reliability and validity tests on the data, and further using the model for hypothesis testing, this paper conducted a descriptive statistical analysis of each measurement variable and each measurement item. The results are shown in the following table.

The average value of the perceived brand is 4.818, and the standard deviation is 1.273. In the measurement item of perceived brand, the average score of the three items is above 4 points, and Q14 – "I will give priority to download sports APP launched by famous developers", has the highest score. These show that users generally have a high evaluation of perceived brands, and they are likely to give priority to downloading sports APPs launched by well-known developers.

The average value of perceived trust is 4.367, and the standard deviation is 1.365. Except Q15 – "I think sports APPs downloaded through mobile phones are safer", the average score of which is 3.857, the other items' are all above 4 points, indicating that users generally have a high perception and trust evaluation of sports APPs.

The average value of perceived trust is 3.601, and the standard deviation is 1.512. Among them, Q18 – "how many times have you purchased the most frequently used brand products of sports APP platform?", the score of which is the lowest-only 1.976, and the average value of other items are between 3.8 and 4.0. It indicates that the number

Table 3. Descriptive statistics of variables

Variable	Measurement item code	Project mean	Project standard deviation	Variable mean	Variable standard deviation
Brand perception	Q12	4.405	1.791	4 .818	1 .273
	Q13	4.238	1.518		
	Q14	4.857	1.449		
Perceived trust	Q15	3.857	1.592	4 .367	1 .365
	Q16	4.774	1.329		
	Q17	4.143	1.39		
Purchase behavior	Q18	1.976	1.456	3.601	1.512
	Q20	3.910	1.624		
	Q21	3.948	1.413		
	Q22	3.974	1.565		
	Q23	3.833	1.390		

of times that users purchase goods in the platform is not much, but their repurchase intention, satisfaction and derivative behavior are generally high (Fig. 1).

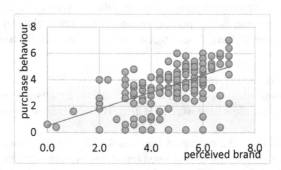

Fig. 2. Perception and brand purchase behavior Scatter

Through further analysis of the relationship between perceived brand, perceived trust, perceived value and purchase behavior, this paper draws a scatter diagram as shown above. As shown in Figs. 2, 3 and 4, perceived brand, perceived trust and perceived value are positively correlated with purchase behavior.

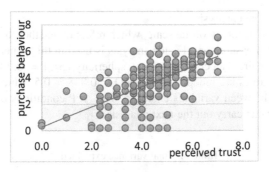

Fig. 3. Perception of trust and buying behavior of the scatter plot

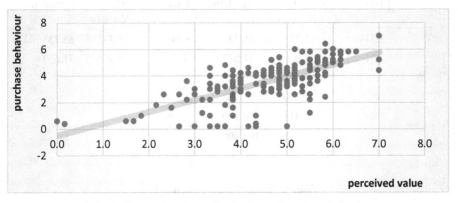

Fig. 4. Scatterplot of perceived value and purchase behavior

5.3   Sample Data and Validity Analysis

Reliability analysis of the sample data
This article analyzes the questionnaire with the SPSS Statistics 26.0.

Reliability refers to the reliability, repeatability, and reliability of the scale's measurement results. The scale is less affected by the environment such as time and place, and the test results are more stable. In this paper, the reliability of the questionnaire is tested using the Cronbach coefficient.

The Alpha coefficient of each measurement item is greater than 0.7. Especially, the alpha coefficient of purchase behavior is 0.908 > 0.9. According to statistical significance, the alpha coefficient is usually feasible between 0.7–0.9, and above 0.9 is considered very credible. It can be seen that the reliability of the overall scale is good.

Table 4. Reliability analysis results

Measurement item	Brand perception	Perceived trust	Perceived value	Purchase behaviour
Cronbach Alpha	0.743	0.800	0.838	0.908

Validity sample data analysis

Validity refers to the accuracy of the scale, which refers to whether the scale can really detect the target of measurement. Factor analysis is used in this paper. For the second part of the questionnaire data correlation test, sphericity test, P = 0.000 < 0.05, which shows that the variables are independent; KMO = 0.838 > 0.5, which shows that the partial correlation between variables is strong. The APP conditions of factor analysis are satisfied, so we can carry out the next analysis.

Table 5. Total variance explained

Component	Initial Eigenvalues			Extraction sums of squared loadings		
	Total	% of Variance	Cumulative %	Total	% of Variance	Cumulative %
1	3.344	55.735	55.735	3.344	55.735	55.735
2	.954	15.902	71.637	.954	15.902	71.637
3	.517	8.611	80.248			
4	.452	7.540	87.788			
5	.385	6.411	94.199			
6	.348	5.801	100.000			

Table 6. Rotated component matrix

Rotated component matrix[a]

	Component	
	1	2
12, I will download sports APPs that are highly rated by others	.084	.866
13, I think the top sports APP is generally launched by well-known developers	.260	.793
14, I will give priority to downloading sports APP launched by well-known developers	.563	.570
15, I think sports APPs downloaded through mobile phones are safer	.668	.504
16, I trust the quality of the sports APP I download	.834	.223
17, I think the sports APP developers in the APP store are reputable	.867	.074

As shown in Table 5, two main factors of perceived brand and perceived trust can be extracted, and the cumulative variance contribution rate reaches 71.637%, indicating that these two factors give a sufficient summary of most of the data. As shown in Table 6, the two factors contain 6 original variables, of which the first three items (Questions 12–14) belong to the first factor (perceived brand), and the last three items (15–17) belong to the second factor (Perceived trust). The variables and measurement items proposed in Table 1 are consistent with this.

5.4 Correlation Analysis

Correlation relationship refers to an incompletely deterministic relationship between phenomena, that is, whether the value of one variable can be uniquely determined by another variable. Correlation analysis is a statistical method to determine whether there is a correlation between variables and to study the relationship strength of the correlation. Through the scatter plot in Figs. 2, 3 and 4, we can find that there is a certain positive correlation between perceived brand, perceived trust, perceived value and purchase behavior. In this paper, Pearson correlation coefficient is used to quantitatively analyze the relationship between variables.

Table 7. Correlation between perceived value and purchase behavior

	Brand perception	Perceived trust	Perceived value	Purchase behaviour
Brand perception	1			
Perceived trust	.581**	1		
Perceived value	. 881**	. 897**	1	
Purchase behaviour	. 538**	. 683**	. 690**	1

As can be seen from the table above, perceived value and its two dimensions (perceived brand, perceived trust) have a certain correlation with purchasing behavior. In addition, the correlation coefficients r of all variables are all greater than 0.5, which is at or above the moderate correlation level.

Table 8. Statistic of each correlation coefficient test

	Brand perception	Perceived trust	Perceived value
Perceived trust	9.787732929		
Perceived value	25.53212456	27.82397	
Purchase behaviour	8.751087873	12.82118	13.07085

Hypothesis H0: $\rho = 0$; H1: $\rho \neq 0$.

According to the significance level $\alpha = 0.05$, looking at t distribution table can get T $\alpha/2$ (190–2) = 1.987. It can be seen from the table that the statistics of each correlation coefficient test t > T $\alpha/2$ (190–2) = 1.987, rejecting H 0, that is, there is a positive linear correlation between each variable.

5.5   Regression Analysis

Regression analysis is based on a set of sample data to determine the mathematical relationship between variables. Respective analysis was conducted using perceived brand, perceived trust, and perceived value (the two variables of perceived brand and perceived trust) as independent variables, and purchasing behavior as the dependent variable. The results are shown in Tables 9 and 10.

Table 9. Linear correlation analysis of each dimension and purchase behavior

Model	DW	R side after modification	Standard estimation error	T	F	Distinctiveness
Brand perception	1.938	.344	5.751	9.851	97.046	.000
Perceived trust	2.034	.550	4.767	14.976	224.292	.000

Table 10. Regression analysis of purchasing behavior on perceived brand and perceived trust

Model		Standardized coefficient
1	Brand perception	.5 90
2	Perceived trust	.7 43

The Influence of Perceived Brand on Purchase Behavior. The regression results show that the F statistic of the model is 97.046, the T statistic is 9.851, and the Sig value is almost 0, which meet the requirements of the F test and T test, so the regression effect is significant. Therefore, the setting of the regression model is acceptable. The revised R^2 is 0.344, indicating that the perceived brand can explain 34.4% of the variation in buying behavior. It is concluded that perceived brand and purchase behavior are significantly positively correlated.

The Influence of Perceived Trust on Purchase Behavior. According to the regression analysis of perceived trust on purchase behavior, the F statistic of the model is 224.292, the T statistic is 14.976, and the Sig value is almost 0, which meet the requirements of F test and T test. The regression effect is significant, so the setting of the regression model is acceptable. The revised R^2 is 0.550, indicating that perceived trust can explain 55% of the variation in buying behavior. It is concluded that perceived trust is significantly positively related to purchase behavior.

The Influence of Perceived Value on Purchase Behavior. The regression results in Table 11 below show that the F statistic, t statistic value of the regression model of perceived value on purchasing behavior are 231.962 and 15.230 respectively, which meet the requirements of F test and t test, and the regression effect is significant. Therefore, the setting of the regression model is acceptable. The revised R^2 is 0.558, indicating that perceived value can explain 55. 8% variation of purchase behavior. The conclusion is that perceived trust is positively correlated with purchase behavior.

Table 11. Partial output results of perceived value and purchase behavior regression

Model		DW	R side after modification	Standard estimation error	T	F	Distinctiveness
Perceived value		2.017	.558	4.722	15.230	231.962	.000
Perceived value (Two dimensions)	Brand perception	2.039	. 580	4.603	3.755	127.266	.000
	Perceived trust				10.152		

In addition, this study attempts to construct the specific functional relationship of the sample regression model. The independent variable selects the perception brand and the perception trust dual variable, and the dependent variable selects the purchase behavior. It can be seen from Table 11 that the D- W value of this model is 2.039, which is located between 1.8–2.2, indicating that the data are independent of each other, which is consistent with the basic assumption of the multiple regression model. A statistical test was performed on the model, and it can be seen from Table 11 that the fitting degree of the model reached 58%, and the explanatory effect of independent variables was significant. At the same time, the model passed the F test and T test, indicating that the sample regression equation fits the overall regression model significantly, and has certain statistical significance.

Further perform multiple collinearity tests on multiple regression models, as shown in Table 12 below. It can be seen that the tolerance of perceived trust and perceived brand is 0.640 < 1, and the variance expansion factor (VIF) < 10, indicating that the effect of multicollinearity between perceived trust and perceived brand is small.

The above analysis results can be obtained by standard regression equation: purchases $= 0\ 225 *$ brand perception $+ 0.608 *$ perception of trust. Through regression analysis, the results of the hypothesis analysis in this paper are shown in Table 12.

Analysis of Gender Regulation

Regulatory variables refer to variables that systematically change the form or strength of the relationship between explanatory and dependent variables, or variables that affect the direction or strength of the relationship between an independent or predictive variable and a dependent or standard variable.

Table 12. Partial output results of purchase behavior on perceived brand and perceived trust regression

Model		Standardized coefficient	t	Distinctiveness	B is 95.0% confidence interval		Collinear statistics	
		Beta			Lower limit	Upper limit	Tolerance	VIF
1	(Constant)		−.843	.400	−3.909	1.569		
	Perceived trust	.608	10.152	.000	.839	1.243	.640	1.562
	Brand perception	.225	3.755	.000	.199	.641	.640	1.562

(1) Gender's moderating role between perceived brand and purchasing behavior.
    Study the impact of perceived brand on purchasing behavior, taking into account the possibility of gender as a moderating variable. Using S PSS data according to the analysis result of the split sex following table.
    Group of males and females in group F statistics were 24.983,0.898, significant resistance were .000 < .05, .349 > .05, the results showed that the regression model females group there was no significregulating trust and purchasing beha-viant linear relationship tested by the estimated standard The error is large, and the regression model has no statistical significance, and it cannot explain that gender has a moderating effect on perceived brand and purchasing behavior.

Table 13. Gender's moderating effects on perceived brand and Purchase behavior

Gender	Model	R side	Adjusted R- square	Standard estimated error	F	Distinctiveness
		.392	.386	6.014	66.992	.000
Male	1	.397	.381	6.541	24.983	.000
Female	2	.021	−.002	6.097	.898	.349

(2) Gender's role in regulating trust and purchasing behavior
    Using the same method to analyze the moderating role of gender in perceived trust and purchasing behavior, the results are shown in Table 14. It can be seen that the regression models of the gender groups are meaningful. Both the F statistic and the significance level have passed the test, indicating that the regression model has a good linear relationship. According to the t test results of the regression coefficients on the perceived trust of males and females, it is found that the regression coefficients are meaningful. Then two regression coefficients need for hypothesis testing, but SPSS does not directly teste two regression coefficients, but may calculate their

re-spective 95% confidence intervals. The results showed that 95% CI of male's coeffi-cient of perceived trust was between .623 and 1.764; 95% CI of female's perceived trust regression coefficient was between.355–1.495, and the confidence interval of male included the confidence interval of female. Therefore, the difference between the two regression coefficients was not statistically significant. Therefore, gender does not have the regulatory effect of perceived trust on purchasing.

Table 14. Gender's moderating effects on perceived trust and purchase behavior

gender	model	R side	Adjusted R-square	Standard Estimated Error	F change	Significant F change
.	1	.780 a	.608	.605	161.567	.000
1	1	.566 a	.320	.303	17.920	.000
2	1	.451 a	.204	.185	10.737	.002

gender	model		Unstandardized coefficient B	Standard error	Standardized coefficient Beta	t	Distinctiveness	B is 95.0% confidence interval Lower limit	Upper limit
.	1	(Constant)	1.688	1.462		1.155	.251	-1.211	4.588
		Perceived trust	1.318	.104	.780	12.711	.000	1.112	1.523
1	1	(Constant)	.960	3.792		.253	.801	-6.716	8.637
		Perceived trust	1.193	.282	.566	4.233	.000	.623	1.764
2	1	(Constant)	4.702	3.674		1.280	.208	-2.713	12.118
		Perceived trust	.925	.282	.451	3.277	.002	.355	1.495

(3) Gender's moderating role between perceived value and purchase behavior
Using the same method to analyze the moderating role of gender in perceived trust and purchasing behavior, the results are shown in Table 15. It can be seen that the regression models of the males and females groups are meaningful. Both the F statistic and the significance level have passed the test, indicating that the regression model has a good linear relationship. According to the t test results of the regression coefficients on the perceived trust of males and females, it is found that the regression coefficients are meaningful. Then perform hypothesis testing on the two regression coefficients to calculate their respective 95% confidence intervals. 95% found that males perceived trust regression coefficients CI:..544 ~ 1.116; male's 95% confidence sensing regression coefficients CI: .030 .630 ~, there is little overlap between the confidence interval, can be described with a certain separation, Therefore, the difference between the two regression coefficients is statistically significant, indicating that gender regulates the effect of perceived trust on purchasing behavior.

In summary, assuming that a, b, c, and f are established, that is, the perceived brand has a positive correlation with the purchase behavior of products on the sports social platform, the perceived trust has a positive correlation with the purchase behavior of

Table 15. Gender's moderating effects on perceived value and purchase behavior

Gender	Model	R side	Adjusted R-square	Standard Estimated Error	F change	Significant F change
	1	.609	.605	4.823	161.825	.000
Male	1	.449	.435	6.250	30.985	.000
Female	1	.105	.084	5.830	4.920	.032

Gender	Model		Unstandardized coefficient		Standardized coefficient	t	Distinctiveness	B is 95.0% confidence interval	
			B	Standard error	Beta			Lower limit	Upper limit
	1	(Constant)	-3.499	1.852		-1.889	.062	-7.171	.174
.		Perceived value	.798	.063	.780	12.721	.000	.673	.922
	1	(Constant)	-5.889	4.111		-1.432	.160	-14.211	2.434
1		Perceived value	.855	.154	.670	5.566	.000	.544	1.166
	1	(Constant)	7.670	4.047		1.895	.065	-.497	15.837
2		Perceived value	.330	.149	.324	2.218	.032	.030	.630

products on the sports social platform, and the perceived value (The dual role of perceived brand and perceived value) is positively related to the purchase behavior of products on the sports social platform, and gender regulates the perceived value of sports APP users on the purchase behavior of platform products. Assume that the verification results are shown in Table 16.

6   Conclusions

Through the research in this article, we can see that the dual roles of perceived brand, perceived trust, and both of sports APP users have a positive effect on the purchase behavior of products on the platform, and of the two, perceived trust has a greater impact. It can be seen from Tables 9 and 11 that the influence of per-ceived brand on purchasing behavior accounts for about 34.4%, and perceived trust accounts for 55.0%. The dual effect of the two is 58.0%. This shows that the more the users of sports APP trust the APPs they use, the more likely they are to purchase the products on the platform.

Table 16. Research hypothesis verification

Research hypothesis	Verification
a: Sports APP user perception brand has a positive impact on platform product purchase behavior	Established
b: Sports APP user perception trust has a positive impact on platform merchandise purchase behavior	Established
c: Sports users perceived value (perceived brand and perceived trust) has a positive effect on platform merchandise purchase behavior	Established
d: Gender regulates the brand perception of sports APP users on the purchase behavior of platform products	Invalid
e: Gender has a moderating effect on the perceived trust of sports APP users on the purchase behavior of platform products	Invalid
f: Gender has a moderating effect on the perceived value of sports APP users on the purchase behavior of platform products	Established

The second is the brand of APPs. If the brand market-ing of APPs is better, there is also a greater possibility that it will promote the user's purchase behavior of platform products.

According to this study, there are the following suggestions for sports APP platform shopping malls: You can market sports APP brands, such as evaluation and ranking, to pay attention to the maintenance of APP's own safety, quality, and reputation.

In particular, sports APP can be marketed through word-of-marketing, as Table 2 shows that in brand perception, the selection criteria of "famous" and "other people's evaluation" have received a large proportion of users Recognition.

When the sports APP platform only focuses on a certain aspect for some reasons, it can increase the purchase volume of users by increasing the user's trust in the sports APP. It can be seen from Tables 9 and 11 that the impact of perceived trust on purchase behavior is around 55%, which is about twice that of perceived brand, and the combined effect of the two only reaches 58%. This shows that with the same effort to increase perceived trust or both perceived brand and perceived trust, the difference between the two is not very large. Therefore, when other conditions are constant, the importance of perceived trust is higher than that of perceived brand.

7 Research Limitations

This study also has some subjective and objective limitations. Subjectively, this study issued a 190-point questionnaire. The subjects of the survey are mainly college students. For a large group of sports APP users, these samples do not reflect the overall situation. On the other hand, the independent variables selected in this study are the subjective perceptions of users, and the suggestions made are relatively abstract. How to connect with the user's actual behavior, such as usage behavior, to provide more specific sugges-tions for the improvement of purchasing behavior, further research is needed. Second, the factors that influence buying behavior very much, very much information, this study explains only about 58% of the reason.

Objectively, affected by the new crown epidemic, the public has greatly reduced the frequency of going out, so the purchase behavior of the goods in the sports APP is also not the same as usual. However, the time when the questionnaire was issued coincided with the period of the epidemic, and some measurement contents were also affected. Intuitive, the third part of this questionnaire on consumer-based survey of this behavior: You buy the latest sports APP platform brand products of the time, because there is no through reliability testing, this issue was ultimately deleted. Although some problems have passed the reliability test, their statistical data may be affected, and it is not intuitively reflected, so some errors caused by the research results are also inevitable.

Questionnaire:

Research on the Impact of the Use Behavior of Sports APP Platform on Users' Purchase Behavior of Platform Products.

Basic Information
1. Gender
Male and Female
2. Age
18 years old and below
18–25 years old
25–35 years old
35–50 years old
Over 50 years old
3. Education background
High school and below
Specialist
Undergraduate
Master's degree
PhD students and above
4. Your monthly living expenses:
A below 1000 yuan B 1000–2000 yuan C 2000–3000 yuan D above 3000 yuan
Sports APP users' movement patterns
5. How do you choose sports APP:
A friend recommended B advertisement C mobile APP store random download D sports community professionals recommended E. Other
6. The sports APP you currently use is (Multiple choices)
Keep, Fit time, Gudong Sports, Nick Run, WeChat(WeChat sports), Huawei Health, Xiaomi Health, Yue moving circle, QQ health Other (Please fill in the specific name)
7. Common sports methods using sports APP
A running, B fitness, C yoga, D walking, E swimming, F mountain climbing, G cycling, H other
Sports APP usage behavior
A Study on the Use of Sports APP by College Students in Changchun City and Its Effect on Physical Exercise Behavior
8. The historical time of your exposure to sports social platforms
A less than a month, B 1–6 months, C 6–12 months, D 1 year -2 years, E 2 years or more
9. How often do you use sports social platforms
A 3 times or more per day, B 1–2 times per day, C 2–3 days, D once a week, E every 2 weeks or more
10. Each time you use sports social platforms
A 30 min or less, B 30 min–60 min, C 60 min–90 min, D 90 min–120 min, E 120 min or more
11. How often do you share sports records on social platforms
A never, B occasionally, C more than three times a week, D daily
Perceived value (perceived brand, perceived trust)
From 1–7, where 1 means you were not agreed at all and a 7 means you highly agree
12. I will download sports APP highly rated by others
1 2 3 4 5 6 7

13. I think that sports APP rankings are generally launched by relatively well-known developers

1 2 3 4 5 6 7

14. I will give priority to download sports APPs launched by more famous developers

1 2 3 4 5 6 7

15. I think by the movement of the mobile phone download APP are relatively safe

1 2 3 4 5 6 7

16. I trust the quality of the sports APP I downloaded

1 2 3 4 5 6 7

17. I think the sports APP developers in the APP store are all reputable

1 2 3 4 5 6 7

Purchase Behavior:

18. How many times have you purchased the most commonly used sports APP platform brand products? (Such as millet bracelet, keep mall light food, godong mall equipment, etc.)

A never B 1 ~ 2 times C 3 ~ 5 times D 5 times or more

19. When was the last time you purchased a branded product on the sports APP platform?

A within one month B within three months C within six months D within one year E within two years F has never purchased

Consumers' willingness to repurchase and satisfaction

20. You are satisfied with the experience of purchasing sports APP platform products

1 2 3 4 5 6 7

21. In the future, if I want to buy such products, I will choose the brand.

1 2 3 4 5 6 7

22. If necessary, I will buy other products of the brand

1 2 3 4 5 6 7

Consumer derivative behavior: customer recommendation, introduction and word-of- promotion

23. I will actively recommend the brand to friends

1 2 3 4 5 6 7

References

1. Huang, M.: Research on the influence of sports APP on sports consumption behavior
2. Chuanhai, L., Qingmei, W., Junwei, Q.: The effect of sports APP on the promotion of physical exercise behavior and the formation of sports habits. J. Nanjing Inst. Phys. Educ. (Soc. Sci. Ed.) **3**, 109–115 (2015)
3. Wang, L., Hu, M., Zhu, W.: Research on the influence of sports social platform on users' behavior of using smart bracelet. 2095–2171 (2017). https://doi.org/10.13365/j.jirm.2017.03.005
4. Lin, L.: Research on the influencing factors of mobile shopping behavior of consumer APP. 713.36:658
5. Dallinga, J.M., Mennes, M., Alpay, L., Bijwaard, H., de la Faille-Deutekom, M.B.: APP use, physical activity and healthy lifestyle: a cross sectional study (2015)

6. Beldad, A.D., Hegner, S.M.: Expanding the technology acceptance model with the inclusion of trust, social influence, and health valuation to determine the predictors of German users' willingness to continue using a fitness APP: a structural equation modeling approach (2018)
7. Xianglan, Z.: Consumer Behavior. Tsinghua University Press, Beijing (2012)

Developing a Smart Personal Health Monitoring Architecture and Its Capacity

Si Li[1], Yichuan Wang[2], and Minhao Zhang[3](✉)

[1] Guangzhou Xinhua University, 7 Yanjiangxiyi Road, Machong Town, Dongguan 523133, Guangdong, China
[2] Sheffield University Management School, University of Sheffield, Sheffield, UK
[3] School of Management, University of Bristol, Bristol, UK
minhao.zhang@bristol.ac.uk

Abstract. To improve healthcare delivery quality and to reduce medical cost of elderly care, healthcare organisations have increasingly adopted smart personal health monitoring system. However, anecdotal accounts of smart personal health monitoring systems' potential benefits realisation are rare. This paper aims to develop a smart personal health monitoring system with the design principles of Event-Driven Architecture (EDA). An EDA is a design method of information technology architecture that uses to detect and monitor asynchronous events and respond to them intelligently by a publish/subscribe mechanism. We define Event-Driven Architecture capacity as Information Systems capabilities triggered by implementation of Event-Driven architecture. Understanding smart personal health monitoring systems by EDA is needed and desirable. We identify four capacities of smart personal health monitoring system: flexibility capacity, sensing capacity, interoperability capacity, and responding capacity that are generated from an event-driven architecture.

Keywords: Smart personal health monitoring system · Event-driven architecture · Health care · Information system capability

1 Introduction

In the healthcare field, the assimilation of health information technology (HIT) has been a surge of interest in understanding how to leverage IT architectures or information systems (IS) to improve healthcare delivery and reduce medical cost effectively in healthcare organisations (Agarwal et al. 2010; Lucas et al. 2013; Mantzana et al. 2007). Among the emerging IT architectures, Event-driven architecture (EDA) has been introduced as a top choice for corporations, particularly for health care organisations (El Sawy and Pavlou 2008), and has been widely used in the healthcare industry (Taylor et al. 2009) to increase organisation performance. EDA's design principles include publish/subscribe architectural messaging, loose coupling between publishers and subscribers and the asynchronous interaction mechanisms (Chen et al. 2011; Mouttham et al. 2009; Taylor et al. 2009). Due to its popularity and effectiveness, software vendors increasingly follow

© Springer Nature Singapore Pte Ltd. 2021
Y. Wang et al. (Eds.): DHA 2020, CCIS 1412, pp. 118–126, 2021.
https://doi.org/10.1007/978-981-16-3631-8_11

EDA's design principles to develop healthcare-related systems such as emerging disease surveillance system (e.g., identifying the COVID-19 pandemic signal or monitoring the confirmed cases), personal health devices, radio frequency identification (RFID) systems and remote healthcare system. One example of such application is the personal health monitoring systems that are developed using the publish/subscribe mechanism within complex event processing. This design helps eliminate human medical errors and provide instant and detailed records of patient's clinical state (Mouttham et al. 2009). EDA-based healthcare systems are regarded as facilitators of productivity or profitability in healthcare organisation, fostering the growth of clinical outcomes, reducing the care delivery costs, and eventually leading to sustained competitive advantage.

Bountiful number of studies on IT adoption or effectiveness and efficiency of IT architectures in healthcare settings exist in the literature while studies evaluating the capabilities and effectiveness of an IT artifact still lacking (Agarwal et al. 2010; Drnevich and Croson 2013; Jones et al. 2012). Despite the current attention on event-driven IT architecture for healthcare prosperity, EDA-enabled IT capabilities remain vague and unmeasured. Given the importance attributed to EDA for a healthcare information system, it is essential that sound research to develop a set of EDA capability be conducted, which serves as the main goal of this study. Specifically, the purpose of this study is to present the development of a multidimensional measure of EDA capability in the personal health monitoring systems.

2   Literature Review

2.1   An Overview of Event-Driven Architecture

The EDA is an IT architectural design method. This system architecture consists of messaging, adapter, message transformation, business flow coordination, event notification and surveillance (Ranadivé 1999; Wang et al. 2013). The EDA-enabled systems are designed based on publish/subscribe architectural messaging, loose coupling between publishers and subscribers and the asynchronous interaction mechanisms (Michelson 2006; Taylor et al. 2009) to provide services. Publish/subscribe mechanism allows detecting asynchronous events or messages and to respond to them automatically. Loose coupling function takes care of operations within interoperable platforms (Taylor et al. 2009; Yuan and Lu 2009). Asynchronous interaction function allows interaction take place not necessarily at predetermined or regular intervals thus increases flexibility. Generally, EDA-based systems involve event publisher, event processing layer and event subscriber embedded in the complex event processing flow. In the EDA-based systems, every event or message will be processed between publishers where the events are detected from various data sources as well as subscribers (also known as event receivers) where the events are received and utilised (Eugster et al. 2003; Luckham 2002). This publishing and receiving process involves event processing rules, historical events for comparison, business process, and users (Michelson 2006). One EDA application example is the vigilant information systems (VIS) proposed by Walls et al. (1992) and subsequently is applied in supply chains by Houghton et al. (2004). VIS is derived from the concept of an observe-orient-decide-act (OODA) loop. This system provides real-time dashboards utilising various sources to detect changes (i.e., observe) and combines event-based alerts for diagnosing and analysing problems (i.e., orient). The information in VIS is sharable to help decision-makers to track and manage activities and processes across functions (i.e., decide and act) (El Sawy and Pavlou 2008; Houghton et al. 2004). As noted, these EDA systems are developed and designed by three key design principles: publish/subscribe mechanism, asynchronous interaction, and loose coupling as visualised in Fig. 1 below.

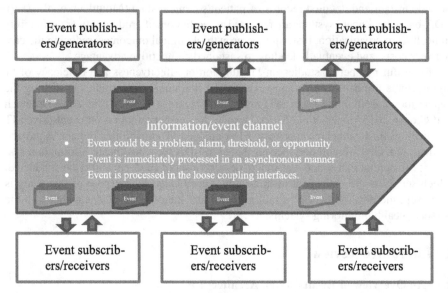

Fig. 1. The design principles of EDA systems

3   Event-Driven Architecture Capacity

IS capability can be triggered by implementation of IS/IT architecture (Chen et al. 2010; Wade and Hulland 2004). From this theoretical standpoint, we contend EDA-based systems as a unique, distinctive IT resource to generate EDA-specific IT capabilities that reinforces capability of an IS system.

Although a substantial amount of IT infrastructure research has indicated the potential benefits of EDA, we encountered a hard challenge to find EDA capacity definitions, let alone an universally accepted definition of EDA capacity or its dimensions. Taylor et al. (2009) define EDA capability as "*the ability to disseminate information immediately to all interested targets by integrating ordinary or notable events happening inside or outside business and further evaluate the event and optionally take action by human or automatic operation*" (p. 16). EDA capacity has also been defined as the complete set of services for moving, managing, and integrating information to trigger productive responses within an event processing mechanism (Ranadivé 1999; Wang et al. 2013). Based on these two definitions, EDA capacity is conceptualised in this study as a multi-dimension construct with more than one conceptually distinguishable facets.

In the context of health care, the definition of EDA capacity is noticeably absent from most articles. We only found Taylor et al. (2009) define EDA capacity in health care as the ability to synchronise the analysis of multiple data streams in real time to detect medical abuse and possible treatment protocols. We define EDA capacity in healthcare setting as *"the ability to propagate the medical events in real-time or near real-time across healthcare units intelligently and to support them to examine patients' condition and then make decisions for treatments appropriately."*

In the healthcare setting, EDA capacity reflects the extent to which a health system efficiently and effectively manages and controls its relevant resources to facilitate the operational processes based on an event-driven architecture. Previous research has focused on the adoption of healthcare devices and the design of EDA framework, as we summarised in Table 1. The formation of IT capability and its benefits from the adoption of EDA-based healthcare systems can be recognized from these studies. For

Table 1. EDA related literature in healthcare

Study	The domain of healthcare	Subject area
AAMI (2012)	General healthcare	An emphasis on how to improve the safety and effectiveness of the diverse array of healthcare IT through medical device interoperability
Chen et al. (2011)	Public health administration	Develop a framework for emerging infectious diseases management by using the loose coupling to detect unusual patient cases
Fitterer and de Witte (2009)	Sickbed management	Propose an event-driven service-oriented architecture for improving the care delivery and performance of back-end processes
Mouttham et al. (2009)	Health monitoring system	Develop an EDA-based personal health monitoring system for integrating healthcare data and validate the proposed architecture by scenario analysis
Singh and Bacon (2009)	Preventative care	Provide a paradigm on the effective use of event-based data dissemination control in healthcare
Taylor et al. (2009)	General healthcare	A brief notion of EDA in healthcare settings and provide an example of complex EDA use in healthcare industry

example, emerging infectious diseases systems that designed by loose coupling among central control and local personnel in public health administration are capable of not only helping recognise clinical needs by receiving early alert events, but also facilitating local hospitals' decision-making and action-taking (Chen et al. 2011).

3.1 Flexibility

One of the EDA capacities is flexibility where it allows an EDA-enabled system or device to adapt operational changes quickly through three architectural principles: *modularity, compatibility, and maintainability*. Modularity is the extent to which an information system's components can be added, modified, separated, recombined, and removed (Byrd and Turner 2000, 2001; Wang et al. 2013). Loose coupling function allows users to connect the nodes, add or remove the logical operations within modules and revise the logical errors in every layer (Taylor et al. 2009). Modularity has the potential to create an agile healthcare system that promptly detects emerging medical events and reduce unexpected medical risks in a short time. In particular, modularity in the smart personal health monitoring system can help care providers to organise health service to heterogeneous patient groups and to support customisation of healthcare provision.

Compatibility is the degree to which various type of information can be shared across IT module packages or IT components (Byrd and Turner 2000; Duncan 1995; Wang et al. 2013). An EDA system with strong compatibility allows data collected from devices to convert into a consistent format for further analysis and use (Ranadivé 1999). A personal health monitoring system demonstrated by Mouttham et al. (2009) is a typical application of EDA system that shows that how compatibility can be applied in the system. When a patient, who wears smart personal health monitoring device, suffers from a health emergency, the device will trigger appropriate response by Message Broker no matter if the response is sent from different health administration domains and then contact a healthcare provider for further actions. Likewise, Zhai et al. (2021) propose a 5G-enabled smart ambulance system to deal with emergency tasks. This smart system connects communication network in the ambulance with remote video communication located in the hospital network. When an accident occurs at the accident scene and an ambulance arrives, this EDA-enabled system can transmit information between emergency department team at the destination hospital and ambulance crews.

Maintainability is rooted in the loose coupling function, enabling systems to have a strong changeability. This ability allows IT component to change without affecting other IT components or subsystems (Taylor et al. 2009; Wang et al. 2013). It is important for a smart personal health monitoring system where sudden errors can be fixed within a module without influencing on entire monitoring system.

3.2 Sensing

Sensing capacity is viewed as an IT architectural ability that enables users to accurately identify events from multiple publishers in real-time or near real-time (El Sawy and Pavlou 2008; Houghton et al. 2004). This ability is crucial for smart personal health monitoring system where real-time information (e.g., unpredictable accidents) can be tracked and gathered. For example, Texas Health Harris Methodist Hospital collects patient data from medical sensors they use to track (or event predict) patients' movements during their stay (Wang et al. 2018). With this ability, EDA system has the potential to alert early risks by monitoring scattered activities (Li et al. 2019; Wang et al. 2013), identify areas for service improvement along with key performance indicators (KPIs) (Houghton et al. 2004; Li et al. 2019), and reduce occurrences of unnecessary costs (Tavakoli et al. 2013). In particular, sensing KPIs in the EDA system environment could help to eradicate losses, acquire new knowledge by analyzing previous errors (Wang et al. 2013) and provide managerial visibility (e.g., KPI dashboard or metrics) into the critical operational processes that help users make sound decisions.

3.3 Interoperability

Interoperability is the extent to which data can be exchanged and shared among two or more IT modules or components (Kuehn et al. 2011; Taylor et al. 2009). In the healthcare context, interoperability is defined as the ability of health information systems (e.g., medical devices and clinical systems) to communicate with each other across organisational boundaries that can advance effective healthcare information delivery for individuals and communities (AAMI 2012; Mead 2006). EDA interoperability includes the ability to connect with external point-to-point interfaces among care service providers, insurance companies, and R&D and pharmaceutical companies, while flexibility focuses on the ability to communicate within internal application-to-application system components.

Figure 2 show the interoperable personal health monitoring system which consists of three architectural components: patients with device, event management mediator, and hospitals. This system transforms the asynchronous patient data (e.g., service requests, self-management data) by the event management mediator. The mediator enables effective communication between patients and host hospitals (Spooner and Classen 2009; Walker and Denna 1997), resulting in effective early detection and prevention of adverse events (AAMI 2012) and reduction of cost and medical errors (Dantu and Mahapatra 2013; Moraes et al. 2013).

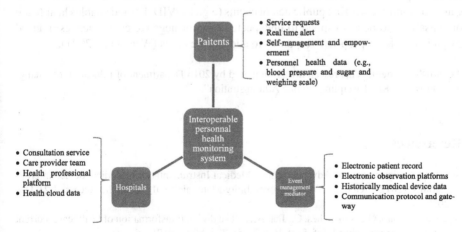

Fig. 2. Visualising interoperable personal health monitoring system

3.4 Responding Capability

Responding capability is one of the IT capabilities that allows IT system to support users' decision-making and action-taking at the organisational level. An EDA system with effective responding mechanism produces sharable knowledge such as various reporting, executive summaries, drill-down queries, statistics analyses, and time series comparisons (Houghton et al. 2004; Wang et al. 2013). These reports enable a user to increase attention and awareness toward events and formulate responding strategies to overcome threats and crises. For example, a remote patient monitoring system developed by the home health system solution providers empowers care service managers and on-duty healthcare professionals to make intelligent decisions based on the triage protocols setting (Singh et al. 2011; Wang et al. 2013).

4 Discussion and Conclusion

Event-driven architecture seems to be dominating the healthcare information system implementation in the healthcare industry to improve clinical and financial outcomes. EDA allows care providers to track patients' events and records in real time, changes rules easily within different health administration domains, implements rules that enable proactive response to future needs as well as incorporates various healthcare information systems for interoperability. However, most of prior EDA research has focused on the technological understanding of EDA rather than recognising the strategic perspectives of EDA. Little is known about the potential IT capabilities to be brought by EDA. Specifically, there is no measurement instrument for EDA that enables healthcare organisations' understanding of EDA-related healthcare technologies in terms of capabilities, functionalities, and effectiveness.

To meet this need for EDA research, this study has identified four dimensions of EDA capability in the case of personal health monitoring system: flexibility, sensing, responding, and interoperability. The overall EDA capability has the potential to provide support for developing personal health monitoring system. Moreover, event-driven architecture can also monitor emerging public health events (e.g., COVID-19) and enables healthcare organisations to better respond to unexpected risks or negative consequences induced by patients with appropriate responses to address the crisis (Wang et al. 2021).

Acknowledgement. This research was supported by 2016 Department of Education of Guangdong Province, Key Discipline "Public Administration".

References

AAMI (Association for the Advancement of Medical Instrumentation): Medical device interoperability (2012). www.aami.org/interoperability/Materials/MDI_1203.pdf. Accessed 21 Dec 2020

Agarwal, R., Gao, G., DesRoches, C., Jha, A.K.: The digital transformation of healthcare: current status and the road ahead. Inf. Syst. Res. **21**(4), 796–809 (2010)

Byrd, T.A., Turner, D.E.: An Exploratory analysis of the value of the skills of IT personnel: their relationship to IS infrastructure and competitive advantage. Decis. Sci. **32**(1), 21–54 (2001)

Byrd, T.A., Turner, E.D.: An exploratory analysis of the information technology infrastructure flexibility construct. J. Manag. Inf. Syst. **17**(1), 167–208 (2000)

Chen, D.Q., Mocker, M., Preston, D.S.: Information systems strategy: reconceptualization, measurement, and implications. MIS Q. **34**(2), 233–259 (2010)

Chen, Y.D., Brown, S.A., Hu, P.J.H., King, C.C., Chen, H.: Managing emerging infectious diseases with information systems: reconceptualizing outbreak management through the lens of loose coupling. Inf. Syst. Res. **22**(3), 447–468 (2011)

Dantu, R., Mahapatra, R.: Adoption of telemedicine – challenges and opportunities. In: Proceedings of the Nineteenth Americas Conference on Information Systems, Chicago, Illinois (2013)

Drnevich, P.L., Croson, D.C.: Information technology and business-level strategy: toward an integrated theoretical perspective. MIS Q. **37**(2), 483–509 (2013)

Duncan, N.B.: Capturing flexibility of information technology infrastructure: a study of resource characteristics and their measure. J. Manag. Inf. Syst. **12**(2), 37–57 (1995)

El Sawy, O.A., Pavlou, P.A.: IT-enabled business capabilities for turbulent environments. MIS Q. Executive **7**(3), 139–150 (2008)

Eugster, P.Th., Felber, P.A., Guerraoui, R., Kermarrec, A.M.: The many faces of publish/subscribe. ACM Comput. Surv. **35**(2), 114–131 (2003)

Fitterer, R., de Witte, B.: Enabling pervasive healthcare by means of event-driven service-oriented architectures: the case of bed management in mid-sized to large-sized hospitals. Pervasive Health, 1–4 (2009)

Houghton, R., El Sawy, O.A., Gray, P., Donegan, C., Joshi, A.: Vigilant information systems for managing enterprises in dynamic supply chains: real-time dashboards at western digital. MIS Q. Executive **3**(1), 19–35 (2004)

Jones, S.S., Heaton, P.S., Rudin, R.S., Schneider, E.C.: Unraveling the IT productivity paradox - lessons for health care. N. Engl. J. Med. **366**(24), 2243–2245 (2012)

Kaye, D.: Loosely Coupled: The Missing Pieces of Web Services. RDS Press, Marin County (2003)

Kuehn, A., Kaschewsky, M., Kappeeler, A., Spichiger, A., Riedl, R.: Interoperability and information brokers in public safety: an approach toward seamless emergency communications. J. Theor. Appl. Electron. Commer. Res. **6**(1), 43–60 (2011)

Li, S., Yu, C.H., Wang, Y., Babu, Y.: Exploring adverse drug reactions of diabetes medicine using social media analytics and interactive visualizations. Int. J. Inf. Manag. **48**, 228–237 (2019)

Lucas Jr., H.C., Agarwal, R., Clemons, E.K., El Sawy, O.A., Weber, B.: Impactful research on transformational information technology: an opportunity to inform new audiences. MIS Q. **37**(2), 371–382 (2013)

Luckham, D.: The Power of Events: An introduction to Complex Event Processing in Distributed Enterprise Systems. Pearson Education, Boston (2002)

Mantzana, V., Themistocleous, M., Irani, Z., Morabito, V.: Identifying healthcare actors involved in the adoption of information systems. Eur. J. Inf. Syst. **16**(1), 91–102 (2007)

Mead, C.N.: Data interchange standards in healthcare IT-computable semantic interoperability: now possible but still difficult, do we really need a better mousetrap? J. Health Care Inf. Manag. **20**(1), 71–78 (2006)

Michelson, B.M.: Event-driven architecture overview: event-driven SOA is just part of the EDA story. Patricia Seybold Group (2006)

Moraes, J.L.C., Souza, W.L., Pires, L.F., Prado, A.F.: Message generation facilities for interoperability in pervasive healthcare environments. In: Proceedings of the Nineteenth Americas Conference on Information Systems, Chicago, Illinois (2013)

Mouttham, A., Peyton, L., Eze, B., El Saddik, A.: Event-driven data integration for personal health monitoring. J. Emerg. Technol. Web Intell. 1(2),. 110–118 (2009)

Ranadivé, V.: The Power of Now: How Winning Companies Sense and Respond to Change Using Real-Time Technology. McGraw-Hill, New York (1999)

Singh, J., Bacon, J.: Event-based data dissemination control in healthcare. In: Weerasinghe, D. (ed.) eHealth 2008. LNICSSITE, vol. 0001, pp. 167–174. Springer, Heidelberg (2009). https://doi.org/10.1007/978-3-642-00413-1_21

Singh, R., Mathiassen, L., Stachura, M.E., Astapova, E.V.: Dynamic capabilities in home health: IT-enabled transformation of post-acute care. J. Assoc. Inf. Syst. 12, 163–188 (2011)

Spooner, S.A., Classen, D.C.: Data standards and improvement of quality and safety in child health care. Pediatrics 123, 74–79 (2009)

Tavakoli, S., Mousavi, A., Broomhead, P.: Event tracking for real-time unaware sensitivity analysis (EventTracker). IEEE Trans. Knowl. Data Eng. 25(2), 348–359 (2013)

Taylor, H., Yochem, A., Phillips, L., Martinez, F.: Event-Driven Architecture: How SOA Enables the Real-Time Enterprise, Addison-Wesley Professional, Boston (2009)

Wade, M., Hulland, J.: Review: the resource-based view and information systems research: review, extension, and suggestions for future research. MIS Q. 28(1), 107–142 (2004)

Walker, K.B., Denna, E.L.: Arrivederci, Pacioli? A new accounting system is emerging. Manag. Account. 79(1), 22–30 (1997)

Walls, J.G., Widmeyer, G.R., El Sawy, O.A.: Building an information system design theory for vigilant EIS. Inf. Syst. Res. 3(1), 36–59 (1992)

Wang, Y., Kung, L., Byrd, T.: Leveraging event-driven it architecture capability for competitive advantage in healthcare industry: a mediated model. In: Proceeding of Thirty Fourth International Conference on Information Systems, Milan, December 2013

Wang, Y., Kung, L., Byrd, T.A.: Big data analytics: understanding its capabilities and potential benefits for healthcare organizations. Technol. Forecast. Soc. Chang. 126, 3–13 (2018)

Wang, Y., Zhang, M., Li, S., McLeay, F., Gupta, S.: Corporate responses to the coronavirus crisis and their impact on electronic-word-of-mouth and trust recovery: evidence from social media. Br. J. Manag. (2021). https://doi.org/10.1111/1467-8551.12497

Yuan, S.T., Lu, M.R.: A value-centric event driven model and architecture: a case study of adaptive complement of SOA for distributed care service delivery. Expert Syst. Appl. 36, 3671–3694 (2009)

Zhai, Y., et al.: 5G-network-enabled smart ambulance: architecture, application, and evaluation. IEEE Netw. 35(1), 190–196 (2021)

From Isolation to Coordination: How Can Telemedicine Help Combat the COVID-19 Outbreak?

Yunkai Zhai[1,5,6], Yichuan Wang[2(✉)], Minhao Zhang[3], Jody Hoffer Gittell[4],
Shuai Jiang[1,5], Baozhan Chen[1,5], Fangfang Cui[1,5], Xianying He[1,5], Jie Zhao[1,5],
and Xiaojun Wang[3]

[1] The First Affiliated Hospital of Zhengzhou University, Zhengzhou, China
[2] Sheffield University Management School, University of Sheffield, Sheffield, UK
Yichuan.wang@sheffield.ac.uk
[3] School of Management, University of Bristol, Bristol, UK
[4] The Heller School for Social Policy and Management, Brandeis University, Waltham, USA
[5] National Telemedicine Center of China, Zhengzhou, China
[6] Management Engineering School, Zhengzhou University, Zhengzhou, China

Abstract. Hospitals are suffering from a critical challenge induced by the rapid spread of Coronavirus disease 2019 (COVID-19). Not only have patients been marginalized, but many clinicians working in the region-al hospitals have limited access to the specialist consultations and treatment guidelines they need from provincial-level hospitals to manage pneumonia cases caused by COVID-19. Telemedicine has been acknowledged as a breakthrough technology in combating epidemics. This study aims to demonstrate the implementation of Emergency Telemedicine Consultation System (ETCS) since COVID-2019 first emerged in Henan Province, beginning in late December 2019. This system was developed for coronavirus care across 126 connected hospitals, serving as the overarching authoritative source for diagnostic decision making and knowledge sharing for treatment. The information shared could rapidly expand to enable open collaborations with key stakeholders such as government authorities, research institutions and laboratories. The experience from building this system during this crisis can provide insights to guide public health institutions as they implement telemedicine to increase resilience to future epidemic outbreaks.

Keywords: Coronavirus (COVID-19) · Telemedicine system · Relational coordination · 5G network

1 Introduction

The rapid spread of Coronavirus disease 2019 (COVID-19) presents hospitals with a critical challenge. As normal capacity of the hospitals is exceeded, healthcare professionals struggling to manage this unprecedented crisis face the difficult question of how best to coordinate the medical resources used in highly separated locations. In China,

© Springer Nature Singapore Pte Ltd. 2021
Y. Wang et al. (Eds.): DHA 2020, CCIS 1412, pp. 127–132, 2021.
https://doi.org/10.1007/978-981-16-3631-8_12

many cities have been imposing a lockdown, due to the high risk of infection and the characteristic of human-to-human transmission (Phan et al 2020). Not only have patients been marginalized, but many clinicians working in the regional hospitals have limited access to the specialist consultations and treatment guidelines they need from provincial-level hospitals to manage pneumonia cases caused by COVID-19. As long as the crisis continues, simply relying on the traditional communicative practices, such as physician office visit or face-to-face consultations within the health professional network, could pose significant costs and health concerns.

Telemedicine has been acknowledged as a breakthrough technology in combating epidemics (Williams and Bisaga 2016). Combining the functions of online conversation and real-time clinical data exchange, telemedicine can provide technical support to the emerging need for workflow digitalization (Andreassen et al. 2015; Lehoux et al. 2002; Nicolini 2006). Previous works have focused on the interaction between patients and the hospital specialists (e.g. Pappas and Seale 2009), studying the patient's expectations of the telemedicine adoption (e.g. Zobair et al. 2019) and policymaking on the telemedicine distributions (e.g. May et al. 2005). Yet, there has been little information on the actual coordination at the inter-organizational level that might help health department in combating the pandemic crisis. Indeed, how the telemedicine may support the coordination across the boundary of hospitals received scant attention (Claggett and Karahanna 2018). Such an omission is unfortunate, as fighting a pandemic requires not only the effective resource allocation but also the flexibility. Although the telemedicine could be promising in offering the flexibility to the coordination within the professional networks, there are challenges of maintaining the communication quality and efficiency of decision making, as the traditional work processes in health coordination is digitally mediated. This raises the question: *How can telemedicine systems operate in a coordinated manner to deliver effective care to patients with COVID-19 and to combat the crisis outbreak?*

2 Emergency Telemedicine Consultation System for Combating COVID-19

Responding rapidly to COVID-19 crisis, the National Telemedicine Center of China (NTCC), located in Zhengzhou, Henan Province, has established the Emergency Telemedicine Consultation System (ETCS), a telemedicine-enabled outbreak alert and response network. Implementation of the telemedicine system is supported by grants from the Novel Coronavirus Pneumonia Prevention and Control Headquarters (NCP-PCH) and the Finance Department of Henan Province. A subsidy of 10 million Chinese yuan has been allocated to the construction and operation of ETCS. Collaborating with China Mobile and Huawei Technologies Co., Ltd., on January 29, 2020 the NTCC sent 18 workgroups to isolation wards to set up telemedicine networks and equipment. The total round-trip distance we travelled was about 9,320 miles, via box trucks, while the approximate round-trip distance to the farthest hospital from the NTCC headquarters in Zhengzhou was 743 miles. Based on our previous experience of building 5G networks and smart medical terminals (Zhai et al 2021), 126 network hospitals were successfully connected to the NTCC on ETCS within 82 h.

ETCS is built upon a doctor-to-doctor (D2D) approach, in which health services can be accessed remotely through terminals across hospitals. The system architecture of ETCS comprises three major architectural layers: (1) telemedicine service platform layer, (2) telemedicine cloud layer, and (3) telemedicine service application layer, as depicted in Fig. 1. *The telemedicine service platform layer* enables a specialist treatment team of provincial specialists to conquer distance and provide access to clinicians working in the regional hospitals. It provides clinicians and patients with immediate diagnosis and consultations regarding COVID-19, wireless remote patient monitoring, remote multiple disciplinary care, and telehealth for education and training, utilizing interactive live video conferencing. The specialist treatment team members work closely with the NCPPCH and Health Commission of Henan Province to prevent and control the spread of COVID-19. *The telemedicine cloud layer* allows clinicians to capture, store and process patient medical records, and to achieve real-time data exchange. In addition, prevention and treatment guidelines, and guidance on drug use and management of coronavirus patients can be accessed via the telemedicine cloud. *The telemedicine service application layer* involves 2 provincial-level hospitals, 18 municipal hospitals and 106 county-level hospitals, which can obtain consultations from the specialist treatment team. This logical structure supports a system of telemedicine clinical management to combat the COVID-19 outbreak.

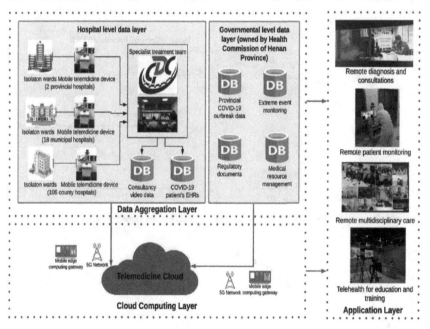

Fig. 1. Architecture of the emergency telemedicine consultation system

3 Performance Evaluation of Emergency Telemedicine Consultation System

Our ETCS has demonstrated substantial benefits in terms of the effectiveness of consultations and remote patient monitoring, multidisciplinary care, and prevention education and training. *First*, 63 severe cases and 591 patients with mild and moderate respiratory infections received telemedicine consultations through the ETCS between January 28, 2020 and February 17, 2020. As of February 17, 2020, 420 cases had been cured and discharged from the hospitals. *Second*, in the isolation wards, the mobile telemedicine device effectively collects, transforms, and evaluates patient health data such as blood pressure, oxygen level, and respiratory rate, and reports them to the care team. This facilitates the avoidance of direct physical contact, thus reducing the risk of exposure to respiratory secretions and preventing the potential transmission of infection to physicians and nurses. *Third*, the specialist treatment team includes specialists from different clinical disciplines and can therefore offer comprehensive assessment and treatment. Meanwhile, nurse care managers and social workers can be involved strategically to help patients with pneumonia obtain post-treatment care to avoid coronavirus re-infection. *Fourth*, the specialist treatment team provides primary care guidance on coronavirus (e.g., clinical criteria for COVID-19 diagnosis, patient transfers, and cleaning process) to all physicians and nurses at 126 connected hospitals via video conference. Substantial

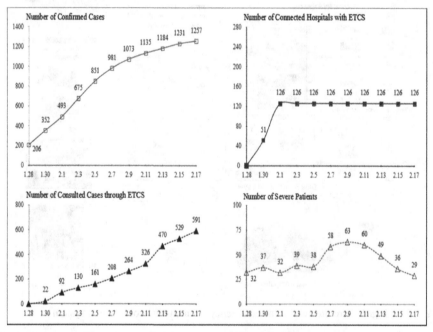

Fig. 2. System performance of ETCS during the COVID-19 outbreak presented by the number of confirmed cases, the number of connected hospitals with ETCS, the number of consulted cases through ETCS, and the number of severe patients reported through ETCS

efforts are devoted to training physicians and nurses, many of whom are new to the treatment of coronavirus infections (Fig. 2).

Notes: 1.28 and 2.17 in the chart refer to January 28, 2020 and February 17, 2020 respectively. The number of consulted cases through ETCS refers to the number of consultations provided by the provincial specialist treatment team to the municipal and county hospitals, excluding the consultations provided by the municipal hospitals to the county hospitals.

4 Conclusion

As we look to the future of epidemic prevention and control, we believe that telemedicine systems have the potential to play a role as surveillance systems in addressing emergencies and large-scale outbreaks in high uncertainty settings (Lipsitch et al. 2020). As telemedicine has inevitably altered the traditional working relationships within the healthcare network, how to ensure high-quality communication among healthcare practitioners poses a significant challenge. As such, frequent, timely, accurate, and problem-solving focused communication among clinical staffs from hospitals at different levels in the healthcare system is essential to minimize the risk incurred in handling patients with possible COVID-19 infection (Gittell 2016). However, we have found that high quality of communication is not always maintained during the telemedicine coordination. Therefore, a learning telemedicine system platform for coronavirus care was developed across connected hospitals, serving as the overarching authoritative source for diagnostic decision making and knowledge sharing for treatment. The platform could aggregate COVID-19 patient records across 126 connected hospitals and rapidly expand to enable open collaborations with key stakeholders such as government authorities, research institutions and laboratories. The lessons learned from this crisis can provide insights to guide public health institutions as they implement telemedicine to increase resilience to future epidemic outbreaks.

For future development of ETCS, we suggest integrating relational coordination practices to optimize the effectiveness of ETCS. Specifically, the key dimensions "relationships" and "communication" rooted in relational coordination theory can be involved into the development of emergency telemedicine consultation system. Over the past decade, relational coordination has been found to facilitate the quality and efficiency of digitally mediated work processes (Claggett and Karahanna 2018). In the healthcare settings, many studies have adopted the relational coordination in building collaborations and examined its impact on health care performance (Khosla et al. 2016). The literature suggests, when facing the rapid spread of an epidemic, delivering high quality of service requires trust amongst stakeholders (Wang et al. 2021). Thus, relational coordination allows us to optimize telemedicine system by building trust through a robust coordination mechanism among hospitals at different levels during the pandemic crisis.

References

Andreassen, H.K., Kjekshus, L.E., Tjora, A.: Survival of the project: a case study of ICT innovation in health care. Soc. Sci. Med. **132**, 62–69 (2015)

Claggett, J.L., Karahanna, E.: Unpacking the structure of coordination mechanisms and the role of relational coordination in an era of digitally mediated work processes. Acad. Manag. Rev. **43**(4), 704–722 (2018)

Gittell, J.H.: Rethinking autonomy: relationships as a source of resilience in a changing healthcare system. Health Serv. Res. **51**(5), 1701–1795 (2016)

Khosla, N., Marsteller, J.A., Hsu, Y.J., Elliott, D.L.: Analysing collaboration among HIV agencies through combining network theory and relational coordination. Soc. Sci. Med. **150**, 85–94 (2016)

Lehoux, P., Sicotte, C., Denis, J.L., Berg, M., Lacroix, A.: The theory of use behind telemedicine: how compatible with physicians' clinical routines? Soc. Sci. Med. **54**(6), 889–904 (2002)

Lipsitch, M., Swerdlow, D.L., Finelli, L.: Defining the epidemiology of Covid-19—studies needed. N. Engl. J. Med. **382**(13), 1194–1196 (2020)

May, C., Finch, T., Mair, F., Mort, M.: Towards a wireless patient: chronic illness, scarce care and technological innovation in the United Kingdom. Soc. Sci. Med. **61**(7), 1485–1494 (2005)

Nicolini, D.: The work to make telemedicine work: a social and articulative view. Soc. Sci. Med. **62**(11), 2754–2767 (2006)

Pappas, Y., Seale, C.: The opening phase of telemedicine consultations: an analysis of interaction. Soc. Sci. Med. **68**(7), 1229–1237 (2009)

Phan, L.T., et al.: Importation and human-to-human transmission of a novel coronavirus in Vietnam. N. Engl. J. Med. **382**(9), 872–874 (2020)

Wang, Y., Zhang, M., Li, S., Mcleay, F., Gupta, S.: Corporate responses to the coronavirus crisis and their impact on electronic-word-of-mouth and trust recovery: evidence from social media. Br. Jo. Manag. (2021). https://doi.org/10.1111/1467-8551.12497

Williams, A.R., Bisaga, A.: From AIDS to opioids—how to combat an epidemic. N. Engl. J. Med. **375**(9), 813–815 (2016)

Zhai, Y., et al.: 5G-network-enabled smart ambulance: architecture, application, and evaluation. IEEE Netw. **35**(1), 190–196 (2021)

Zobair, K.M., Sanzogni, L., Sandhu, K.: Expectations of telemedicine health service adoption in rural Bangladesh. Soc. Sci. Med. **238**, 112485 (2019)

Author Index

Printed in the United States
by Baker & Taylor Publisher Services